BIGGER
THAN ME

HOW A BOY CONQUERED DYSLEXIA
TO PLAY IN THE NFL

By
Jovan Haye
with M.M. Buckner

This book is dedicated to

everyone who continues to dream

despite obstacles like dyslexia.

Published by
Haye Publishing
Nashville, Tennessee

Design & Layout by
Mickey Payne, Third Wave Designs
Terri Morris, Mollie B Creative, LLC

Editor: Phyllis Gobbell

ISBN: 978-0-615-89879-7

First Addition: October, 2013

Printed in the United States of America

TABLE OF CONTENTS

ACKNOWLEDGMENTS

Many people have helped me find my way through life, and without them, I would not have a story to tell. First and foremost are my wife Jennifer Haye and our two lovely daughters, Jorielle and Jaiana. Particular thanks go to my brother Michael Haye, who has always been my biggest fan.

I also want to thank the many people who raised me, including my parents Michael and Jacquelyn Haye, as well as my aunties, Dell, Peaches, Cynthia, Dawn, Madge, Dahlia, and Velma, and my uncles, Richie, Man, Barry, Dean, Robin, Woody, Howie, Dennis, and Tony. Thanks to my many cousins, including Audia, Neshia and Kendra, and to my grandparents. I appreciate all my extended family in Jamaica, New Jersey, and Florida. I also owe thanks to Jennifer's parents, Debby and Gary, Jimmy and Wanda, and to her siblings, Matt and Jamie, for their encouragement.

Thanks to two extraordinary high school teachers, Mrs. Knight and Mrs. Patton, who helped me let go of dyslexia and learn other ways to learn. Also thanks to my compassionate professor at Vanderbilt University, Dr. Brian Griffith, and to my extremely helpful advisor, Mrs. Elizabeth Wright. In addition, I feel profound gratitude to my friends in "2-Trill" who accepted me for who I am: Cheron, Kelechi, Moses, Dominique, Keith, Jerrin, Ronnie, and Brandon.

Countless football coaches recognized my talent and helped me improve over the years. Among them are

"Rock" Nelson, Joe Redmond, Bobby Johnson, David Turner, Ryan Fowler, Jon Gruden, Todd Walsh, Monte Kiffin, Jim Washburn, and Jeff Fisher. Thanks also to the Tampa Bay Buccaneers General Manager Mark Dominik and to their former scout and close friend, Mike Martin. I want to thank all the scouts, coaches, trainers and staff I've worked with at the Carolina Panthers, Cleveland Browns, Tampa Bay Buccaneers, Tennessee Titans, and Detroit Lions, as well as my former agent, Jack Sharf, and in particular, my current agent, Sean Kiernan.

I've been blessed to know and work with Ramon and Juan Alvarado, my business partners in postsharesell.com. We're looking forward to a promising future, serving small businesses and consumers coast to coast, and someday, around the world. Special thanks go to Mary M. Buckner who helped me write this book. She and I share the hope that this story will inspire others to reach for their dreams.

To list every person who deserves my gratitude would take another book, but each one of them is in my heart. Finally and most importantly, I want to thank God for guiding my steps each day.

AUTHORS

Jovan Haye is a former NFL defensive tackle who has lived with dyslexia his entire life. Though he did not start playing football until his junior year in high school, he earned first-team All-State honors as both a junior and a senior. He also graduated with a 4.5 grade point average and earned a scholarship to Vanderbilt University. During his college football career at Vanderbilt, he started every game but one, recorded excellent statistics, and was twice voted team captain.

He was drafted by the Carolina Panthers in the sixth round of the 2005 NFL Draft. He also played for the Cleveland Browns, Tampa Bay Buccaneers, Tennessee Titans, and Detroit Lions. This experience gave him intimate insider knowledge about the NFL, and it also spurred him to find solutions for his various dyslexia-related impediments. Currently, he is part-owner of postsharesell.com, an online exchange devoted to serving businesses and consumers. He lives in Nashville, Tennessee, with his wife and two daughters.

M.M. Buckner is the award-winning author of five novels and is currently at work on a new multi-book series for Penguin/Razorbill. Her work has appeared in five languages, earned a national award, and made the Barnes and Nobel Top Ten in its category. Buckner holds a Master's in Creative Writing from Boston University. She is co-founder and senior editor of TurnStyle Writers, where she teaches, coaches and edits new writers. She has co-written two memoirs.

Other publishing credits include creative nonfiction, magazine features, blogs and content for many websites. In addition, she is a freelance marketing writer, and her advertising copy has earned two Diamond Addies, three NAMA awards, including Best of Show, numerous Golden Quills and other professional tributes. Buckner lives in Nashville, Tennessee with her husband and one cat named "Trouble."

PROLOGUE

We are part of something bigger than ourselves.

Even now, I sometimes wonder how I did it.

Looking back on my childhood in rural Jamaica, I see a
barefoot little kid bouncing around like a wind-up toy, stuttering
constantly, unable to read, and I have to think: Who would have
guessed I could go so far? Only 9 in 10,000 high school senior
football players eventually join the National Football League,
according to the NSAA, but those statistics don't say anything
about football players with dyslexia. As I think about that little
Jamaican kid who hadn't even heard the word *dyslexia* but
understood a lot about the dyslexic life, I know that my story
is one I need to tell.

Dyslexia has many faces, and I've experienced most
of them. One of my odd symptoms is extreme "right-handedness," and on the football scrimmage line, this asymmetry
interfered with my stance. But by the time I came up against
this particular obstacle, I had learned how to find ways
around many others. So I figured out how to compensate
by accelerating my footwork. The dyslexic life is all about
trying harder, preparing more in advance, and finding
work-arounds. I've mastered many techniques, but it took
me a long time to master my fear of what other people
might think about me.

Playing professional football was my dream since middle school, when I first saw the distant stadium lights and heard the cheering fans at a game that I was not allowed to attend. I wanted to be part of that experience, but my mother was dead-set against it. She saw only how dyslexia limited me, not what I might accomplish. In an odd twist, though, my desire to prove to her what I could do was fuel for my journey to the NFL. When I finally played football in high school, my performance earned me a scholarship to Vanderbilt University, where I received my degree. I realized my NFL dream – but from the moment I entered the NFL draft, I became paranoid about revealing my dyslexia, knowing that pro ball players could be cut for any reason.

Take basketball player Royce White. An outstanding power forward, White was named NBA Big 12 Newcomer of the Year when he joined the Houston Rockets, but when they learned he had an anxiety disorder which caused fear of flying, he was suspended and pushed down into the development team. Motion-related phobias are highly correlated with dyslexia, and like Royce White, I also suffered panic attacks in airplanes, especially when we hit bumps. But I didn't let my coaches see.

And there was Rex Ryan, head coach with the New York Jets. He must have known the risks when he admitted having dyslexia at a national press conference. Ryan had a proven record of coaching success. He had led the Jets to two AFC Championship games. But when he "came out" about his dyslexia, he was so nervous that he started stuttering. I knew exactly how he felt. Too many people think dyslexia means "slow-witted," while, in fact, researchers haven't found any link between dyslexia and IQ. But they have found links to a host of surprising complications, like fear of flying.

I've made it a point to learn all I can about dyslexia. I've discovered that my childhood speech impediments and attention deficit hyperactive disorder, or ADHD, as well as visual processing disorder, dyscalculia and dysgraphia, anxieties, and phobias may all be associated with the same genetic mutations that caused my dyslexia. In my low-income neighborhoods, my underfunded schools and even my home, I endured loneliness, ridicule, and violence because of my condition. That was a big part of what drove me to prove that I was not merely a "dumb kid."

I gave a huge effort to become an honor roll student and then a college graduate, but more than anything, I became a student of football. I had so many setbacks that sometimes all that kept me going was pure love of the game.

No wonder that in my first four years as an NFL defensive lineman, I kept my dyslexia a secret. I was not about to risk everything, not after all I had done to get where I was. Then somehow word about my condition reached a teacher at a private school for children who "learn differently." She asked if I would speak to her kids, and I was happy to say yes. I didn't know she would contact my team's public relations department. That's how my coaches found out. It could've been the end of my pro ball career, but by the time they learned about my dyslexia, my coaches had seen what I could do on the field. I was lucky. Their attitude toward me didn't change.

These days, I have no regrets about "coming out." I've spoken to learning-challenged students many times since that teacher first invited me to her school. Talking to kids has meant a lot to me. I tell them how playing team sports helped me understand that I was part of something bigger than myself, and how that gave me the confidence to achieve my driving ambition. I tell them how important it is to take advantage of educational opportunities. I encourage them to persevere. The average NFL career lasts about three years, and I played for seven. Now my cleats are hanging on my wall, and I'm starting the next phase of my life, launching a new business and spending more precious time with my growing young family.

As I write this, I am thirty years old, and I still have dyslexia. One of my current symptoms is a mild form of obsessive-compulsive disorder, or OCD. Researchers are finding new links between these two syndromes. In my case, I have to switch off the TV, the stove and the lights again and again, even though I can see they're already off. It's the same with water faucets. I keep pushing the lever long after the water stops running. When I grind my teeth, I have to grind each side exactly the same amount, and if I snap my fingers on one hand, I have to immediately snap them on the other hand. When I'm changing my daughter's diaper, I always close the left Velcro first, and if by chance, I do the right one first, I have to start all over. Funny little habits, right? But these routines don't hinder me. I just find them interesting.

Now I know a lot more about the condition I've struggled with, all my life. The World Federation of

Neurology defines *dyslexia* as a disability in reading, despite instruction, intelligence and opportunity. But the truth is, not even experts agree what dyslexia is. It's often used as a catch-all term covering many different problems. True, the most familiar symptoms relate to reading. Blurry words, reversed letters, doubling, shimmering and shaking are a few of the experiences people report. Writing can be just as difficult, with mixed-up letter and word order. And some people have trouble recognizing images as well as words.

A few years ago, researchers at Wake Forest University found hard evidence that dyslexia is a multi-sensory integration disorder, not just a problem with reading. A person with excellent hearing might still have trouble processing the sound of different words and remembering them later. This leads not only to poor listening comprehension but also to speech disorders, such as delayed speech, stuttering and cluttering. Cluttering means speaking too fast and jumbling the word order. I experienced all of these issues as a child.

Some people with dyslexia find themselves easily distracted by background noise or bright lights. Still others have poor visual processing, meaning that even with 20/20 vision, they have trouble distinguishing foreground from background, forms, size, or positions in space. My own visual processing disorder made it almost impossible for me to score basketball goals, despite perfect vision and hundreds of hours of practice. Researchers are still unearthing other dyslexia complications. The confusing part is that many of the various symptoms can come together – but not always.

What most everyone agrees about is that stress makes dyslexia worse, and I can tell you, every child with dyslexia feels stress.

This book is for all the people who live with a "difference" such as dyslexia – and for all who do not – because everyone needs to understand. I'm no celebrity, and I make no claim to scientific expertise. My story simply illustrates that an obstacle like dyslexia is not a game stopper. Everyone faces challenges of one sort or another, and there is value in being tested, facing defeat and having to start over.

I've come to believe we are all part of something bigger than ourselves. I believe that, regardless of the obstacles, if we tap into the power of a great dream, and if we're willing to keep trying and never give up, we can win. That's why I'm telling my story.

CHAPTER ONE

When We Have No Light, It's Easier To See The Stars

I was born in paradise.

The place was Toll Gate, Jamaica, an easy-going little town far out in the countryside, surrounded by sugar cane fields, canals and blue mountains. My grandpa named me Yovan Pierre Haye, but my name got mixed up on the birth certificate, and the Y got changed to J. Still, to this day, all my Jamaican relatives call me Yovan or Yo.

My mother, Jacquelyn Virginia Beezer, had a reputation as an excellent seamstress. She was a hard worker, an ambitious young woman. One year after my birth on June 21, 1982, she moved to New Jersey and left me with Auntie Dell and our big family in Toll Gate. When I was two, she returned to marry my father, Michael Anthony Haye. I don't remember the wedding, but their wedding photo shows my mother in a white lacy dress with puffy sleeves and a white wide-brim hat covered by a white veil. My dad wears a three-piece pinstripe suit with a white bow-tie. My mother has taken off her glove so that my dad can place the ring on her finger. They are a handsome couple, both tall and slender, with striking features. In that photo, they are both smiling.

As for me, I was content to stay in Toll Gate with Auntie Dell, while my parents made a home in New Jersey.

Auntie Dell was not really my aunt, but she took care of many children in Toll Gate. She was older than my mother. She had gray hair and a compassionate heart, and I loved her. Everybody loved Auntie Dell. I remember her kitchen, the table covered in dishes, pots of soapy water, and the drain board. From the kitchen, we could look out on the chickens running in the yard, laundry hanging on the line to dry, an old tire propped against a crate, cinder blocks and paint cans, where someone was starting to build something. All of that in the middle of incredible natural beauty – palm trees swaying, lush green everywhere.

Many aunts, uncles and cousins lived near us. Auntie Peaches, whose real name was Hortense Haye, was my father's sister. She lived with her brother, my Uncle Richie. Their house stood close to Auntie Dell's, and I spent a lot of time with them.

All the children went in and out of each other's houses constantly. Every child got whippings in Toll Gate. That was normal. When we caused trouble, any nearby adult would whip the whole bunch of us. And sometimes when I got home, Auntie Dell would give me a second whipping for the same deed.

Auntie Dell's house was always full of children, mostly cousins. In our gang of cousins, I was the youngest, and they all remember how I stuttered. My relatives say I used to talk up a storm, but I jumbled my words, so they couldn't understand me. My older cousins laughed at me and mocked the way I talked. So after a while, I began to keep to myself. Sometimes I snuck away to eat dirt. I ate a lot of dirt in those years, and whenever anyone caught me, I got a whipping.

All of our family was big on church, and especially Auntie Dell. From sunset Friday to sunset Saturday, we were not allowed to watch TV or play, because Saturday was the seventh day, the Sabbath. I thought everyone in the world attended the Seventh Day Adventist Church. Our Sabbath meetings lasted three hours, and our family never missed. We lived only a few hundred yards from the church gate. We had to wear shoes and our best clothes. In an old photo, I am a small, slender boy leaning slightly to one side, wearing a starched white shirt, a blue vest, matching trousers, and lace up blue shoes – my Sabbath clothes. My dark eyes are huge and round.

Our church sat square in the middle of Toll Gate. The building was small and simple, white brick with a red corrugated metal roof. The steps had no railings, and at that time, there were holes in the walls. Although we had six jalousie windows and four ceiling fans, the heat inside could be intense. Our two preachers stood behind a simple wooden altar carved with a cross, and behind them was a raised baptismal pool. We sat twenty to a bench, and I used to marvel at all the colors in our single stained-glass window above the pulpit. My attention was easily diverted.

For the first hour, the kids had to attend Children's Bible Study. I didn't like that part because I had a hard time keeping still and quiet. I felt a constant urge to talk, yet I couldn't form a normal sentence like other kids my age. Our teachers made us recite verses, and I couldn't do it because of my stutter. When it came time to say prayers, I was terrible. I just couldn't pay attention.

At that time, I doubt that anyone in Toll Gate had heard of dyslexia or ADHD. The adults must have thought I was being stubborn or defiant, because they yelled at me a lot, and the leader often struck my hand. When things got bad, I withdrew into myself and just stared out the window. It was like I was there, but I wasn't there. Whenever possible, I snuck out and waited till Bible Study was over, then snuck back in and joined Auntie Dell for the main service.

The part of the service that I loved was the gospel music. Our church had a piano and a small choir, and sometimes they brought in drums. My favorite hymns were "When the Saints Go Marching In" and "Onward Christian Soldiers." Those songs gave me goose bumps.

After the service, our congregation often ate together in the church. People would bring dishes of rice and peas, goat, ox tails and fish. Sabbath dinner was a feast. When we returned home, we'd take off our church clothes and hang them up, then sit together and try to keep quiet.

"What verse did you learn today?" Auntie Dell would ask in her soft Jamaican patois.

She'd look straight at me, and she always gave me the sense that she had eyes everywhere. The only thing I could do was clamp my mouth shut and shrug my shoulders.

"You don't remember your verse? Not even a few words?"

I shook my head.

"Did you sneak out of Bible Study again?"

"N-n-no," I lied.

Auntie Dell gave me a frown, and I knew what was coming.

"Go break off a switch, Yovan. Bring it to me right now."

Aunt Dell didn't hit me hard, but her whippings stung more than my skin. I hated that I disappointed her. Afterward, I had to keep sitting on the porch. Till sunset, all we could do was talk, read Bible stories, or take a nap because it was the Sabbath. For me, those long Saturday afternoons were agony.

The rest of the week, though, we ran and played in the wide open fields from early morning till after dark. Nobody worried about crimes or kidnapping. Everybody's door stood open. We'd eat our meals wherever the tastiest food was being cooked, and it was common for us to stay over in each other's houses for days at a time.

We sometimes played with the goats in the sugar cane fields, or we walked up into the mountains and played near the bauxite quarry. We made toy cars from juice boxes bound with banana leaf string, with lemon slices for wheels. We played marbles, hopscotch and hide-and-go-seek. Another favorite game was "gun war." We'd use an old knife to cut guns out of pieces of wood, and then we'd play gun war all day long. In Toll Gate, it didn't take much for kids to have fun.

Livestock roamed as freely as we did. We had chickens, goats, cows, pigs, dogs, and cats. People raised livestock for home consumption, though sometimes they sold goats. The woods and fields were full of tiny Doctor Birds with long twin tails, as well as vultures, egrets, storks, pelicans, ibises, flamingos, too many birds to count. My cousins grew vegetables, herbs, and banana trees in their yards, and they also grew spices like nutmeg, Jamaican red and yellow pepper.

All the buildings in Toll Gate were single story, wood or brick, with metal roof shingles that rusted in the Jamaican sun. The houses were painted blue, green, yellow and brown, and many of them needed repair. Some had no glass in the windows, some had wooden shutters, and some had jalousie windows with narrow glass slats that turned on louvers. Some of the windows were covered with ornamental iron grills, and several front porches featured decorative iron gates.

There were no cell phones or internet in Toll Gate, and few people had cars. If we needed to travel, we caught buses or small vans that operated like taxis. Many people worked in the nearest large town, May Pen, so they commuted by bus. But not everyone had a set job. Many were self-employed as handymen. They did odd jobs, whatever was needed.

We might see adults sewing and rocking on their porches, but they mostly let us be. They gave us only one iron rule: "Stay out of the street!" In Toll Gate, our side streets were made of packed dirt, but the traffic route between May Pen and Mandeville ran right through the middle of Toll Gate. We had no speed limit, and sometimes the vehicles zoomed by so fast, you couldn't tell what color they were. My dad's mom was killed by a car when Dad was a little boy. He held her hand as they carried her to the hospital where she died. I don't think he ever recovered from that.

I remember the graves in people's yards. By tradition, people often buried their loved ones at home. My dad's mother was buried near his childhood home in nearby Almonds. Her vault was made of concrete, and its lid stuck up about two feet above the ground, like a platform. We used to sit on her grave to eat our mangoes. People told us not to sit there, but we never stopped.

Small as it was, Toll Gate had an elementary school that went through eighth grade, and then the kids had to go some-where else for high school. Our little town also had a butcher shop, a small restaurant, and a few local stores. Simple open-air stalls, called "bars," were situated along the main road, in front of the owners' houses. Some of my cousins owned little bars. They might sell anything from ice cream to jerk chicken. The chicken stalls stood right next to the owner's chicken coops. We also had an ice cream man on a motorcycle and many, many good cooks. Everybody cooked.

My favorite foods were ackee-and-salt-fish, fried or boiled dumplings, plantains and bananas. I also loved gizzada, a Jamaican pastry filled with coconut, brown sugar and vanilla, and when we could, we bought bulla cakes or bun-and-cheese at the store. Jamaican cheese came in thick round wheels, so we'd slice a hefty chunk to go in the bun. I also loved red snapper, which was raised in a fish farm not far from Toll Gate.

If we got hungry and there was nothing to cook, we'd munch on sugar cane or fresh fruit. I was a big climber. I could climb any tree to get fruit or just to look around. We had fruit trees everywhere – mango, apple, sour-sop, pear, almond, coconut palm, ackee. One of my favorites was guinep, a small green fruit with pink sweet-sour flesh. We were free to help ourselves, but if we came home with fruit stains on our shirts, we'd get whipped.

In one small market that carried mostly Jamaican products, people shopped for meat, flour, soap, toothpaste, and other staples. We'd spread the toothpaste on a cloth to clean our teeth. Toothbrushes were rare, and they were mainly used to polish shoes for church.

I had only two pairs of shoes, both for church. The rest of the time, I went barefoot like all the other kids, except for a few of my cousins who wore flip-flops. Today, when I walk barefoot on rocks, my feet hurt – but not then. We roamed carefree over grasslands and mud, through the forest and up the hills. If we stepped on a prick, we just pulled it out and kept going. Many times I cut my feet on barbed wire, but I never worried.

Mosquitoes ruled Jamaica. They bred in the canals and gullies that crisscrossed the fields, an old irrigation system left over from plantation times. I was always covered in bites. I got lots of poison ivy, too, and I can still smell the calamine lotion Auntie Dell smeared on my skin.

Morning and night, we took showers outside in a stall made of corrugated metal open to the sky. Sometimes we took showers in the rain. There was no hot water, but that was OK in Jamaica. Auntie Dell had no air conditioning, no fan, just "whatever God gave us." That was her expression. Thanks to the natural Jamaican breeze, that was OK, too.

Nights were very dark. There were no street lamps or lighted shop windows, only stars. We could see a million stars. And when the moon came out, it was right there, like a giant blue disk. Our house had one light bulb in the kitchen, and to light other areas, we burned kerosene lamps.

Watching TV was a treat, though our black-and-white TV had only one channel. I liked cartoons, "Tom and Jerry" and "The Pink Panther." We also watched local news and Jamaican shows, plus "Days of Our Lives" from the States. I guess there were white people on that show, but our TV made them look gray. At that time, I didn't know people came in different colors.

At harvest time, the cane fields were set on fire, and a sweet haze of smoke would hang over our town. The fire burned away the weeds and killed any prowling snakes, so the workers could then cut the cane with machetes. Us kids, though, we never worried about snakes when we raced through the sugar cane. Jamaica has seven species of snakes, none venomous, and I never saw any of them. I think the mongooses kept them away. I often saw mongooses at night behind our house. They looked something like ground-hogs. They were brought over from Africa in the late 1800's to kill Jamaica's rats.

A rich planter owned many of the cane fields around Toll Gate, and his large house stood on a hill above town. Once we went up there and stole some oranges from his grove, and he shot at us with a gun. We could hear the bullets hitting the ground as we fled.

Way back behind one of his cane fields was a stream, maybe eight feet across. The stream was full of broken bottles, which we often stepped on while we played. We caught fish and freshwater shrimp with our bare hands, or sometimes we used scoops made from juice boxes. The fish were small, two or three inches long, and the shrimp were tiny. Still, we'd bring them home to cook. None of us kids had money. The only thing I knew about money was that the Jamaican coins and bills looked pretty. So instead buying expensive cooking oil, we had to steal it from some relative's kitchen. Can you see us, a pack of kids building a fire and throwing our fresh catch into a pan of sizzling oil? But oh, those fish and shrimp were tasty. We ate them whole.

Besides games, we also had arguments and fights, often with no adult supervision. When it came time to do battle, I took my punches like the rest. The girls hit as hard as the boys. They grew up strong, and they held their own. All the kids in Toll Gate grew up tough.

I remember those early childhood days with a smile. Sure, my dyslexic condition caused some problems, but nothing like I'd face later.

During those years, I hardly ever heard from my parents. They must have stayed in touch with Auntie Dell and sent money, but phone calls from the States were expensive, so they never spoke to me. I didn't understand at the time that they were trying to make a better life. If I thought about them at all, in my childish heart, I guess I believed they didn't want me. Why else would they go away and leave me behind?

For me, Toll Gate held everything a person could want. Life was good in paradise.

CHAPTER TWO

No Paradise On Earth Is Permanent

I was about to turn five years old in June of 1987. My aunts were going to give me a birthday party – my very first birthday party – and my parents were coming from New Jersey. I hadn't seen them in two years, and now they had a baby, just two months old, named Michael DeSilva Haye, Jr. All the family was excited about the visit from my parents and my new little brother. I knew *about* them, but I didn't *know* them. To me, we could have been talking about distant relatives. My real attachment was to Auntie Dell, the main person who was raising me.

My dad walked with a limp. Years later, I learned he'd almost died in a fire. He and some others were working in an empty apartment in New Jersey, and they didn't realize the liquid used to coat the wooden floor was releasing a flammable gas. The pilot light on the kitchen stove sparked an explosion that set my dad on fire, and he had to jump from a fourth-floor window. The fall shattered bones in his hips and both legs, and he was badly burned. His entire lower body had to be reconstructed with skin grafts, several surgeries, and dozens of screws. To this day, he still carries those screws in his legs.

I didn't know any of that in 1987. All I knew was that he picked me up and hugged me. Mom hugged me, too, but I felt no special connection to either of them. As I remember, my family never displayed a lot of affection. Jamaican families tend to be very tight-knit, and we feel deep loyalty for each other, but we rarely let it show. We don't like to show pain either. My people are hard-headed, hard-working, and tough. Those are the traits Jamaicans value.

Still, when I look back, it seems strange to have had so much family and to remember so little affection. I'm trying to make things different for my own children. My wife and I hold our daughters and hug them every chance we get, and they never have to doubt that they're loved.

A few days after my parents arrived in Toll Gate, I turned five years old and it was time for my first little birthday party. A crowd of aunts, uncles and cousins gathered on the porch at Auntie Peaches' house to eat. Jamaican parties are all about food and family and telling stories, and we had plenty of all three. I have a few snapshot-memories of that day, but mostly what I remember is the happy feeling, knowing that my birthday was the reason for all of the celebration.

Uncle Richie was out in the yard, cooking a goat. He was a great cook, who made the tastiest curried goat of anyone. A skinny, dark man, dripping with sweat as he cooked, Uncle Richie was kind hearted and protective of all us kids.

My cousins and I hung out in the yard, watching him work in the open air kitchen. It was a simple arrangement, a zinc counter under a shed roof, open on three sides. At that time, the stove was an open fire ring, and the running water came from an outdoor pump a few yards away, which was shared by several families. It may sound rustic, but that was all the kitchen Uncle Richie needed to create a feast.

As usual, I was buzzing around in constant motion, talking to myself. Our neighbors had a barbed-wire fence, and when Uncle Richie saw me climbing it, he yelled for me to get down. We all spoke Jamaican patois, but the gist of what he said was, "Do like I say, or you feel my belt."

I knew he meant it, so I got down and went to play with some puppies that were just learning to walk. Pretty soon, Auntie Peaches came rushing out to get some water. She was a small, light skinned woman with short hair and a very soft voice. In patois, she said, "Yovan, wash your hands. We eat soon."

I put down the puppy and stuttered a mishmash of words, but Auntie Peaches didn't stop to listen. She was always busy, working full time in May Pen and raising a child alone. That day, with her house full of guests, she never stopped moving. It was hot, as usual, so she wore shorts and sandals. She said something to Uncle Richie, then rushed back inside with her water bucket.

When she was gone, I dipped my hands in the wash basin we kept beside the house. Then I dried them on my britches and ran over to watch my older cousins play marbles under a tree. On the porch, we could hear Uncle Dave and some of the others arguing about who was the fastest midfielder on the Jamaican Football Team – or soccer, as the game is known in the States. Uncle Richie loved to argue, so he shouted his opinions from the yard. Mom and Dad mostly listened. They'd been given the best chairs since they were guests. Meanwhile, Auntie Dell was hurrying around with a pitcher of rum punch to refill everyone's glass.

At about six p.m., with the June sun still high in the sky, the meal began. The goat was perfectly done. All the other dishes were arranged on the zinc counter. We filled our plates and sat down in the shade. The rich aromas of curried goat, rice and peas, boiled dumplings and boiled banana made it hard for us kids to wait, but we were not allowed to start eating till Auntie Peaches said a prayer. After that, we were quiet for a while, enjoying the food. I can still taste the juicy goat, seasoned just right.

Then Uncle Richie started telling a funny story about a reggae singer. I didn't get it, but everybody laughed. Uncle Dave knew another story, and that started an argument about who was the best reggae singer in Jamaica, which led back to who was the best Jamaican football player. Even though our national team had won the Caribbean Cup five times, everybody seemed always frustrated by their performance.

All the kids were seated on the ground, and while the adults argued about sports, my cousins and I got into a shoving match. We were always getting into something. I yelled my nonsense language at them, and then one of the older boys started mocking the way I talked, which made me furious.

"Stop dat," Auntie Peaches said in her soft patois. But Auntie Dell came over and slapped all of us.

"Yovan, be nice," my mom said from her chair.

Uncle Dave was sitting next to my dad. Uncle Dave was always sharply dressed, with gold chains and rings. People called him a ladies' man. Dad liked to wear gold, too, so they were talking about a new pinkie ring Uncle Dave had just bought. Auntie Peaches frowned and took their empty plates out to the yard to be washed. I remember that she always seemed a little on edge. Maybe she was just always tired from working so hard.

It wasn't till after the meal that the best part of my birthday party began. Auntie Dell brought out a real cake with a candle burning in the center. She'd baked it herself. It was a white cake with vanilla icing, the first birthday cake I'd ever had. For a few minutes, I became the center of attention. Before that day, if I was the center of attention, it was because I was in trouble – or because people were making fun of me. But this was different. It was wonderful.

My mom said, "Make a wish, Yovan. Then blow out your candle."

I'd never heard of making a wish before, and I wasn't sure how to do it. I don't know what I wished. But I had plenty of help blowing out the candle. Then we all got a big piece of cake with sweet creamy icing.

Next, something even more fantastic occurred. I got a present. This was a true surprise, because Jamaicans are not big on giving gifts, not like people in the States who wouldn't think of a birthday party without gifts. I imagine my round eyes got even bigger as Uncle Richie pointed out one of the roosters running around in the yard and said, "Starting now, dat one belong to you."

I couldn't believe it. I'd never had my own pet before. This bird was a real beauty, tall and proud, with a scarlet comb, silky golden hackles, red and orange side feathers, and a glistening black tail. I went out that minute and started petting him. I named him "Rooster," and for several weeks after that, I carried him around, fed him dried corn by hand, and cheered for him whenever he got into a squabble with the other roosters. My Rooster was a feisty bird. He came out on top every time.

Then one day, Rooster disappeared, and I never saw him again. I know now that he must have gone into somebody's cook pot. Why else did our family raise chickens, except to eat? But losing my pet was hard on me, and not since I was five years old have I ever owned another pet.

My parents went back to New Jersey with my baby brother after their brief visit. I can't say that I missed them. My life got back to normal, those carefree times running through the fields, climbing trees, and fishing in the canals with my cousins. This was all I had ever known.

But everything was about to change.

Auntie Dell was smiling. She must have thought it was good news for me when she said, "Yo, your mom and dad are coming back to take you home."

Home? Toll Gate was my home. I didn't want to go anywhere. I didn't want to leave Auntie Dell and my cousins. I had a little fit.

In her soft patois, Auntie Dell tried to soothe me. "You don't want to go with your mom and dad to a new place?"

"I'm not going!" I cried.

"Poor child, Lord bless his soul," Auntie Dell said, as I lay on the floor, fighting the thought that my parents were going to take me away from Jamaica forever.

CHAPTER THREE

The World Is Bigger Than We Know

When people left Jamaica, they went to a place called "foreign." We pronounced it "farrin." I'd never seen a map. I didn't know Jamaica was an island. No one had told me the earth was round or that a continent lay across the water to the north. I had no idea how I would get to "farrin," or who lived there, or what I would eat. It made me feel sick to think about leaving Jamaica.

Waiting through those last two months was torture. Sometimes, I would sneak away and cry where no one could see me. My stutter grew worse. I felt nervous and ill. During the day, my older cousins would tell me about the big cities and tall buildings I'd see. They were trying to ease my mind, but I couldn't imagine what they meant. The largest buildings I'd seen were the tourist resorts in Negril and Ocho Rios. Everything I knew about "farrin" came from watching "Days of Our Lives" on black-and-white TV.

My parents and baby brother came to get me in August. On the morning we had to leave, Auntie Dell got up early to help me pack my little suitcase, and we stood around in the sun with my aunts, uncles and cousins, hugging and saying goodbye. "Take care, Yo. See you next time," they said, but I didn't know if I'd ever return.

Parting from my cousins was the hardest. They were my best friends. I'd learned all my mischief from them and had all my best laughs as well. But although they were all older than me, on that morning, they stood clinging to each other, crying. "We'll miss you, Yo," they said.

I mumbled goodbye. That day, I cried only on the inside.

A close family friend drove Dad, Mom, little Michael and me to the Norman Manley Airport in Kingston. I'd been there a few times to meet visitors, but I'd never stepped inside. We always waited out on the sidewalk by the line of taxis and hotel buses. I'd never even had a good look at an airplane.

This time, though, we walked through the front door, and I discovered the airport was beautiful. It had cool, sweet-scented air conditioning and reggae music and tropical décor, but there were also uniformed police and soldiers carrying assault rifles. This was serious, I realized. I was really leaving.

No doubt I had too much nervous energy that day, so Dad took me upstairs to look out at the runways. Despite everything else, I fell in love with airplanes that day. Air Jamaica's jets were amazing, with blue, pink, orange and yellow stripes down the sides and a stylized Jamaican Doctor Bird on the tail fin. I pressed against the window to watch the airplanes take off.

When our flight was called, we walked across the scorching black tarmac to climb aboard. The Air Jamaica jet was gorgeous inside, too. Rainbow-colored seats and upholstery, attendants dressed in tropical uniforms – it was like a magic place. Later during the flight, they served real Jamaican ackee-and-salt-fish, plus jerk chicken. The pilot spoke over an intercom, and although his English sounded different from our Jamaican patois, I understood most of what he said. I didn't have a window seat, though, and every time the air grew bumpy, I tensed up because I didn't know what was happening. The strange motion made me uneasy. Eventually, I fell asleep.

We flew about four hours non-stop to New York City. But whoa! The JFK Airport was nothing like the one in Kingston. I expected to walk down a run of stairs to the tarmac like before, but instead, we stepped into a kind of hall on wheels – the jetway. Inside, the airport corridors were enormous, cold, and crowded. I'd never seen so many people in one place. And a lot of them were white.

Believe it or not, I'd never seen white people. Among the crowd, there were also Asians, Africans, Indians and Arabs, people from all over the world wearing all kinds of clothing and speaking in languages I didn't understand. My eyes opened wide.

We had to walk a long way to get our bags and go through Customs. As my parents pulled me along, I stared out the windows at dozens and dozens of airplanes. We passed large bright wall screens listing columns of blinking figures. I couldn't read them, but they astonished me. Next I was amazed by the number of baggage carousels. The Kingston Airport only had one. Also, the police wore a different kind of uniform, and there were no soldiers. I walked very close to Dad, and for once, I didn't make a sound.

Auntie Dawn met us in the baggage area. "Welcome home, Yovan!" She hugged and kissed me, and I was surprised to learn that we had other relatives living in "farrin."

When we walked outside, suddenly there were more cars than I ever knew existed. Acres of parked cars glittered in the sun, and more cars zoomed along the roads. We piled into the family Honda Accord, and as we pulled into the stream of traffic, I wondered why the steering wheel was on the wrong side. Worse, the roads had too many lanes, and the cars drove in the wrong direction.

As we passed the New York seaport, I saw huge ocean-going freighters tied to the wharves. Between the buildings, there were green fields, but no sugar cane, no bananas, no palm trees. Tall buildings glimmered in the distance like a mirage. The size and scale of everything, the numbers of cars and people, the large signs, the overhead traffic lights, every detail confused me. Truly, I'd arrived in "farrin."

Riding in the back seat, I tried to make sense of this new world, but I was tired, lonely and scared. Somewhere in my suitcase, Auntie Dell had packed my marbles, my one memento from home. Oh gosh, I missed Jamaica.

My parents lived in Teaneck, New Jersey, and when we finally pulled up to our home, I saw another parking lot full of cars. Six multi-story buildings were grouped around a circle of clipped green grass, and each building had long rows of windows.

Mom pointed to one of the upper windows. "That's our apartment, Yovan. We live on the fifth floor."

Apartment? I didn't know that word. I didn't know people could live stacked on top of one another. But one detail did catch my eye. In the circle of grass, a few kids were playing on some kind of brightly colored equipment. I later learned the items were called slides, swings and a merry-go-round. I didn't know what they were, but they intrigued me.

Across the street were a lot of stores, but they were entirely different from the ones in Toll Gate. Instead of open-air stalls, these stores had glass windows and closed doors. Some had flashy yellow and red signs. McDonald's. KFC. I'd never heard these names before.

We climbed the stairs to the fifth floor, and I saw light bulbs everywhere. A dozen doors lined the hallway. I thought we lived close together in Jamaica, but that was nothing compared to this cramped apartment building.

Dad turned the key in the lock, and I rushed into my new home. It was air conditioned – just like the airport!

And it was crammed full of family. Auntie Dahlia, her brother Uncle Woody, and her daughter Kendra stepped forward to welcome me. It turned out they lived in the same apartment complex as we did.

Auntie Dahlia kissed me on the cheek. "What a big boy you've grown!"

"Go play with Kendra," Mom told me.

While the adults chatted, cousin Kendra showed me the wonders of the apartment. She was the same age as me, and I felt comfortable with her. First, we explored the main room, a combination kitchen and living room. I ran everywhere and looked in every corner.

Whoa! My parents had a stove inside the house. They also had a sink with hot running water, plus a bathroom with a hot shower and a toilet. Kendra showed me how to work the taps. Every room had electric lights, and she showed me the switches but warned me not to touch.

The other two rooms were bedrooms, one for my parents and baby brother, one for myself and visitors. I bounced on my new bed to test the springs. Then Kendra sat down beside me, and we grinned at each other. All at once, I remembered that strange playground equipment outside. In my overexcited way, I mumbled, "Let's go out and play."

Kendra said we had to ask permission, but when we asked my mom, she shook her head. "Not now. We're talking to our visitors. Maybe tomorrow."

That's when I discovered "farrin" had more surprises in store. Kendra explained that we weren't allowed to go outside by ourselves because New Jersey had kidnappers. We had to wait till an adult was available to watch us.

That night, I tossed in my new bed and listened to the rustling of my new starched sheets. As tired as I was, I couldn't sleep. "Farrin" was kind of exciting, but it didn't feel like home. I kept thinking about running free through the sugar cane fields anytime I wanted, climbing trees with my cousins, picking ripe mangoes and guinep. Those days were gone. I was five years old. My life was over.

CHAPTER FOUR

Sometimes Our Only Defense Is Humor

There was no specific hour or day when I realized my speech made me different from other kids. In Jamaica, my cousins mocked my stutter and laughed at my mixed-up words, but all of us cousins teased each other for all sorts of reason. At least I felt among friends and family in Toll Gate. But very soon after I arrived in Teaneck, I began to comprehend that I was different.

On my second day, Mom finally took me outside to the playground, and the first thing I noticed was that every kid was wearing shoes. I was shocked. All the kids in our apartment complex were black like me, but they were American, and they didn't speak Jamaican patois. They talked like the people in "Days of Our Lives."

When I tried to talk to those American kids, my words came out too fast or not at all. Consonants were like walls to climb, and vowels stretched out too far. Even the simplest words tripped me. Dog, for instance. I'd say ddd-ooooooooog. My Jamaican accent only made the trouble worse.

For the first minute or two, the kids listened and tried to make out what I was saying. Then they lost patience and laughed. But their "farrin" laughter sounded colder than what I'd heard in Toll Gate.

A few days later, Mom drove me to a big blocky institutional building where I had to undergo a school placement test. All kids from Jamaica had to go through that test when they first immigrated to the States. The test was verbal, and I understood the questions pretty well, but I struggled to answer. Words kept jumping around in my head, and my stutter got worse and worse. I didn't do well enough to start first grade. They held me back in kindergarten.

That afternoon, Mom took me for a walk down the street near our apartment, and I stared at the plate-glass shop windows. Teaneck's streets and sidewalks were made of concrete, not earth like in Toll Gate, and the long aisles in grocery stores filled me with awe. Teaneck had a large Jamaican population, so we found familiar foods on the shelves. But Mom didn't buy much. On that first trip, we just bought Jamaican beef patties, a kind of turmeric-yellow flour pastry stuffed with spiced ground beef. I was just beginning to understand that money was tight.

When we got home, Mom assigned me a list of chores. I had to wash dishes, but that would be easy because, unlike

Jamaica, our apartment had indoor running water – and it was already hot. I also had to take out the trash in plastic bags. That seemed weird because in Jamaica, we burned our trash. Every Friday night, my cousins and I would pile up all the trash, douse it with kerosene and toss in a match. Then we'd stand around the fire, waiting for the glass bottles to explode. Many a time I cut my feet on broken glass, but those exploding bottles were cool.

The only fun I had with the trash in Teaneck was trying to sling the bags up into the dumpster behind our building. I was a little guy, and those bags were heavy. First I had to drag them downstairs. Then I'd try to gauge the height of the dumpster and swing the bags up in a high arc over the rim. Sometimes I missed, and the bags would split, drenching me in garbage juice. What a joke on me.

Thinking back on my first day at kindergarten, I'd say it was like landing on a hostile planet. Our local public school was a massive two-story structure with hundreds of kids in grades K-12. The older kids looked like scary giants to me, and all the kids looked alien. For one thing, they were mostly white, and for the first time in my life, I experienced the isolation of being in a minority. Also, unlike Jamaican students, these kids wore no uniforms. They wore stylish "farrin" clothes. More than that, they had a different way of moving, speaking and behaving. They were Americans, and I was not. I felt disorientated.

My parents walked me to my classroom the first day. I took a seat, and despite my habitual tendency to chatter, I don't think I spoke a word. The teacher seemed like a nice lady, but nothing she said or wrote on the board made sense to me. My parents had forewarned her about my stutter, so at least she didn't call on me. The only things about school that I liked were lunch and recess. I sat enduring the minutes till I could meet my cousin Kendra and go home.

As time wore on, I learned to hide in the crowd. Shyness became my protective shell, and at recess, I would find some corner to sit alone, watching the other kids and quietly talking to myself. They all seemed to know each other, and even in kindergarten, small cliques had developed. I watched from a distance, trying to figure them out and worrying that I would never fit in.

That's how I passed through kindergarten into first grade. I didn't learn to read. The alphabet gave me fits, and my penmanship was illegible. I could not stay between the lines or draw the letters correctly. My dad helped with my homework whenever he had time, but my progress reports showed far more frowny faces than smiley ones. Obviously, I fell behind, but there were no tests in kindergarten, and it was rare for teachers to fail students at that age. So my teacher passed me on.

Sometime during my first grade year, we moved to the top floor of our building and joined households with Auntie Dahlia to save money. My cousin Kendra and my maternal grandmother also lived with us. Sharing a home with many relatives was a common thing in Jamaica, and I liked it. Even though Kendra was a year ahead of me in school now, she understood my language, and we soon became allies.

With so many people living together, our apartment was crowded. Sometimes I slept on the couch, sometimes with Grandma, and Michael slept in a bassinet in my parents' bedroom. We had a number of relatives in Teaneck, and we visited back at forth, so I was hardly ever alone at home. At school, though, I was always alone.

My first-grade class work didn't improve. Written symbols looked like gobbledygook to me, and numbers gave me as much trouble as letters. They just didn't have any meaning. Even then, no one suspected dyslexia. The adults simply thought I was "slow," and that's what I thought, too. I was a slow, dumb foreigner who couldn't read or write or even talk. When I brought home my report cards, Mom would yell that I didn't work hard enough, or didn't care, and she would whip me with a belt. The more she struck me, the more furious she'd get.

Studies have found a close link between attention deficit hyperactive disorder and dyslexia. When I look now at a list of ADHD symptoms, it's clear I displayed almost all of them during my youth. There's no doubt that my constant motion and lack of attention stressed my mother. She worked long hours as a nurse's aide in a retirement home, and every day she'd come back exhausted. Plus she did housework, laundry, shopping and cooking. She had little patience with me.

Dad was more understanding, and he had more time. He could no longer do physical labor because of his injured hips and legs, and though he'd applied for disability payments, his case had not yet been settled. So for several years, he worked at a shelter for abused kids called The Center. He drove them on field trips, and sometimes he brought them to our play-ground. I liked to hear their stories. They'd lived through tough times, and Dad was a natural guardian figure for them.

My favorite days were Saturdays, especially in wintertime when it snowed. I loved the snow. Kendra and I would jump down the steps and throw snowballs, and my little brother Michael would toddle around, clapping his hands, with the snow up to his knees. I was always happiest when I could run free and make as much noise as I liked.

A few kids in our apartment complex had sleds and snow saucers, and sometimes they'd let Kendra and me take a ride. There was a nice hill nearby, and we'd slide down till the sleds made deep ruts and the snow got a funny smell from the dog poop underneath.

Saturdays were fun, even when it wasn't snowing. Mom was off from work, so we'd go to church with Grandmother. For a long time, I had believed the Seventh Day Adventist Church was the only religion in the world, but in Teaneck, I began to notice that many people attended church on Sundays, not Saturdays, and instead of keeping quiet on the Sabbath, our neighbors went out to restaurants or parties. I'm sure this influenced my family to be less strict.

Teaneck's Seventh Day Adventist Church wasn't as colorful as in Jamaica. Their music lacked the exciting spirit of our Toll Gate hymns, but on the other hand, Mom didn't make us go to Children's Bible Study, and we didn't have to sit still all afternoon. After church, Mom would take Kendra and me window-shopping. We'd skip up and down the main street near our apartment, looking at everything for sale. We always stopped to admire the shoes in PayLess. Saturdays were our carefree days. I didn't have a worry in the world.

But then Sunday would come around, and I would already feel the shadow of Monday morning. I could never fully enjoy Sunday because I dreaded going back to school.

Every morning before Kendra and I walked off to school, Mom fixed us each a bowl of Chex. It was always plain Wheat Chex, not Cheerios, Cocoa Puffs, Lucky Charms, not even Cinnamon Chex. The grocery store carried lots of other cereals, but I couldn't get Mom to try them.

Mom was always in a rush in the morning, so she poured milk over our Chex while we were still getting dressed. By the time we sat down to breakfast, our cereal was soggy slime that tasted like wet cardboard. Kendra and I both hated it, but Mom insisted that we eat it all.

For a while, we forced it down. Sometimes we'd just tip up our bowls and drink the milk, leaving the gooey Chex behind. But Mom got mad when we did that. She'd say, "I spent good money on that food. Don't waste it!" Then she'd make us sit back down till we finished every bite.

Going without breakfast would have been much better. The Chex made me gag, and Kendra made an awful face every time she put the spoon in her mouth. We thought about throwing the nasty stuff in the garbage, but Mom would only find it and whip us.

One morning, while Mom and Auntie Dahlia were in another room getting dressed, I got Kendra's attention, lifted my bowl and nodded toward the open window. Kendra smiled back at me. Then she got up, tiptoed to the door and kept watch while I dumped our cereal out the window. When Mom came back, our bowls were empty, and we were all grins. Yeah!

We continued this strategy for two weeks. Every morning, we'd wait for the right opportunity. Then Kendra would stand guard while I opened the window and hurled out the mushy Chex. Once, Auntie Dahlia came in and said, "Mercy, you finished that cereal fast."

"We were really hungry," Kendra said.

We never got caught. We were in the clear. Until the day the downstairs neighbor knocked on our door. When Auntie Dahlia answered, the man said, "Who's been throwing cereal out your window?"

"What?" She glanced at us, and my heart jumped. Kendra and I looked at each other.

The man said, "Every morning, I see milk and cereal splattering against my window, and there's a big mess on top of my air conditioner."

"I don't know anything about that," Auntie Dahlia told him.

Mom must have heard, because she came rushing in, scowling. "What kind of cereal?"

I braced for the worst because I knew what the man would say.

"Chex. You can see it for yourself on top of my air conditioner."

Mom wheeled around, put her hands on her hips and glared at me. "What have you been doing?" she said. Of course, she assumed I was the trouble-maker, not Kendra.

"It w-w-wasn't us," I said.

"Are you sure?" she kept saying. "Are you sure?"

I was desperate. I had to try something, so I stammered out a lie. "S-s-somebody above us d-d-did it."

Mom jerked me out of my chair and dragged me to the window. "I'm going to give you one last chance. Did you throw your breakfast out the window?"

I shook my head.

"All right," she said, "look out the window and see who's above us."

I stuck my head out and looked up. All I saw was the sky. How could I have completely forgotten that we lived on the top floor? When I looked down, sure enough there was a sickening mess of dried-out Chex covering the top of the man's window air conditioner. I looked back at Mom I knew I was about to die.

As soon as our neighbor left, Auntie Dahlia spanked Kendra, and Mom walloped me with the belt. She was beside herself, screaming. She didn't stop hitting me until she had to leave for work. But she wasn't finished.

"Just wait till tonight," she said.

All day long, those words followed me around. Nothing else mattered, not school work, not the playground. I dreaded going home. When school let out, Kendra and I walked side by side down the pavement, dragging our feet. We had to go down a hill, then back up another hill, and we walked as slowly as we could. The last part felt like climbing Mt. Everest. I had to force myself to knock on our apartment door.

As soon as Mom opened the door, she grabbed my shirt, pulled me inside and beat me again. "Liar!" she kept shouting as she swung the belt. "I can't believe you wasted my money!"

When Dad came home, he might have given me another whipping, but he could see the welts on my legs. He didn't lay a hand on me. Kendra didn't get a second whipping, only me. Still, I can't help but see the humor of it. To this day, Kendra and I joke about the Chex. If only I had looked down before throwing it out, I could have aimed it to the side and missed the neighbor's air conditioner. I could've gotten off scott free.

CHAPTER FIVE

With Time, Our Scars Become Armor

The person who most often watched over Kendra and me when we played outside was Grandmother, my mom's mother. She had short gray hair and glasses, and she always wore a dress, never slacks or shorts. She was staunchly religious, and the whole time she lived with us, we never missed church. She remains in my mind as a shadowy, distant figure. Near the end of my first-grade year, she died.

She'd been sick for a while, though I didn't realize how bad it was. I now know she had breast cancer. The day she died, Kendra and I were in school. My teacher came to my desk and said, "Get your things together, Jovan. Your parents are here."

I didn't know what was going on till we were outside in the car, driving to the funeral home. Mom said the whole family was flying back to Jamaica in a few days

for Grandmother's funeral service. Jamaica, that's all
I needed to hear. I was going home.

My first flight back to my homeland felt somber and
strange because of Grandmother's death, yet I couldn't wait
to run free with my cousins through the cane fields again.
A crowd of friends and relatives arrived for Grandmother's
funeral. They all wore suits and dresses, and a lot of them
were crying. I had to wear my white shirt and bow tie.
All the little kids peeked into the casket for one more look
at Grandmother, but I didn't want to look. This was the first
funeral I'd attended, the first dead person I'd ever seen, and
the crying adults upset me.

Our church was filled to overflowing, and after the
service, we went to Auntie Peaches' house for a big feast.
People stayed late into the night, and some, like us, stayed
for several days. I spent every free minute playing outside,
splashing in the canals and climbing trees to pick fruit. Then
almost as quickly as we'd rushed down to Jamaica, we rushed
back north to Teaneck so my parents could return to work.

The highways in Jersey, the concrete buildings and
sidewalks, and the endless rows of stores appeared dreary
and gray after my brief visit to paradise. The rest of that
summer passed in a blur. And then came second grade.

My new teacher started sending weekly progress
reports to my parents, and every report earned Mom's anger
and a whipping. Second-grade students were supposed to
read, and I could not do it. I couldn't write the alphabet
properly or put my numbers in the correct order. Though I

often jabbered, I couldn't speak in complete sentences. My words came out jumbled, and I continued to stutter.

No one seemed to understand, or even question, why I had so much difficulty with language – least of all me. People simply called me "dumb." But language wasn't my only difficulty. I was easily distracted and couldn't focus on one thing at a time. I fidgeted and squirmed and wanted to touch everything in sight, and I had trouble processing simple instructions.

Also, I couldn't figure out how to interact with the American kids. I watched what they did, how they talked and teased each other, but I couldn't get the knack of it. I wanted to play like everybody else. I just couldn't understand what made me an outcast.

Looking back, I realize that I'd become so convinced of my own stupidity that I probably stopped trying. More and more, I retreated into my shell. I daydreamed and talked to myself. The teacher complained that she couldn't get me to listen, and she was right. I wasn't there.

Fridays were the worst. That's when I had to bring my latest progress report home. Mom knew the report was coming, so I couldn't hide it. She would take one look at the columns of frowny faces. Then she would yell and throw things, punch, slap, and beat me with a belt. She accompanied each blow with curses and vulgar insults, including the F word, and I learned to stand still and take it. That's probably the reason I'm so tough and strong now. Pressure and pain are nothing to me.

But that year, I cried. My legs were so covered with welts that I couldn't wear short pants. I even began to plot ways to steal the teacher's smiley-face stickers so I could put them on my reports, though I never actually did it. Sometimes I wanted to disappear off the face of the earth.

Eventually, my parents met with my teacher, and I can guess what she told them: Jovan cannot learn. Mom and Dad had always argued a lot about money, but during that time, their arguments centered more and more on me. Often I overheard their loud stormy shouting, and I would cover my ears.

Then one morning, something happened to interrupt the routine. I was walking up the hill to school. For some reason, Kendra wasn't with me that day, and just as I came within sight of the playground, a stranger pulled up beside me in a station wagon. He was white, about thirty-five years old, with long straggly hair and a little brown beard. I'll never forget his face.

"Come over here," he said.

When I approached, sure enough, he showed me a bag of candy. "Have some."

By this time, I must have been eight, and I'd been warned about strangers. I shook my head and backed away.

"Come on, get in the car," he said. "I'll give you a ride to school."

I looked up the hill. My school was only a block away. Right then, I knew the guy was looking to do me harm.

He must have seen my suspicion because he got out of the car and came straight for me.

I ran. That day, the hill didn't exist. I sprinted all the way up the street, into the school, into my home room, and immediately told the teacher what had happened. She took me to the principal's office, and I sat there shaking while they called the police. They also called my parents. When the police arrived, they made me describe the man, and right in front of me, a sketch artist drew his picture. Mom and Dad took time off from work to come get me. I thought for sure Mom would beat me, but that day, she didn't. We were all scared.

Next day, the principal called a special assembly to remind all the kids about not talking to strangers. Then he called me up and presented me with a certificate for saying "No" to a stranger and reporting it right away, the two most important rules. I felt proud of that certificate. That one thing, at least, I had done well.

However, my school work showed no progress. Every day I fell farther behind. Then half-way through my second grade, without warning, my parents jerked me out of school. They had decided I might do better in Toll Gate because the teachers didn't put up with nonsense. If you gave a wrong answer, you got a slap. I suppose they thought the firm discipline of the Jamaican school system would straighten me out.

Sure, I wanted to go back to Jamaica – but not to attend school. Nevertheless, Mom and Dad packed me off in March, and before I knew it, I was flying all by myself on the Air Jamaica jet. This time, Auntie Cynthia met me in the airport in Kingston. Auntie Dell no longer had room for me because some of her grown children had moved into her house. So my parents had arranged for me to stay with Auntie Cynthia.

She was actually my cousin, not my aunt. She was also a hard-working single parent who believed in the usefulness of discipline. I found that out the first day. She was very strict, not only with me but with her two daughters, Audia and Neshia, who were a few years older than me. Their father was not around, and she supported all of us by working every day in May Pen. She also took care of her elderly mother who lived in the same house with us.

Auntie Cynthia was always a little harried, a little overworked, and when we didn't do things to suit her, she whipped us with anything she could grab hold of. She didn't curse, though, or say things to humiliate us, and her whip-pings were not severe. They didn't feel like personal attacks.

I'm sure my parents sent Auntie Cynthia money. Still, I respect her for taking me in and looking after me. She enrolled me in school, bought my books and got my uniform ready. She made sure I was clean, healthy and well fed. She treated me like one of her own.

The Toll Gate All-Age School operated year-round, so I re-started second grade, and from March through August, Auntie Cynthia sent me off to class every day with a lunch pail and a book bag. Jamaican classes were harder than those in the States. There were no coloring books, no play time. If you needed extra support in class, it came in the form of the belt. They never heard of "time outs." If you misbehaved, you got whipped till you bled. Also, the teachers didn't send progress reports, only final grades.

One thing I'll say about the kids I knew in Jamaica, they grew up book smart. I've never met so many smart kids. They did their lessons because punishment would be swift and harsh if they didn't. Jamaican people, especially people in the Seventh Day Adventist Church, placed a high value on education.

At the beginning of every school day, we had to sing the Jamaican national anthem, and I couldn't learn it. As punishment, the teacher made me sing it by myself in front of the whole class, and when I mixed up the words, she hit my hand. Many days I'd come home with my hand as red as a crayon from getting hit.

After the national anthem came the daily prayer, and one prayer stays burned into my memory to this day. The teacher made me stand up in front of the class to recite it. I stuttered all the way through, and everyone laughed at me the entire time.

In reading class, we often read Bible stories. I liked the stories, but I hated the class. Of course I couldn't read. The words on the page jumped around from one line to another, and the letters flipped back and forth. When my turn came, I often just kept my mouth shut, and of course, that earned me a whipping.

The first week, I developed a crush on a little girl in my class. I can't remember her name, but she was slender and pretty, with big brown eyes. I sat right behind her, and all day I would stare at her, too shy to speak.

Then, after a couple of weeks, the teacher separated our class into two groups. Our classroom was divided in half by long chalk boards, and she put good students on one side, dunces on the other. She actually used that word, "dunces." You can guess where she put me. That was the most humiliating day, when the girl I loved saw the teacher move me to the dunce side. I was devastated.

But even with the dunces, I couldn't keep up. When I had to write on the board, my efforts drew snorting laughter from the students and punishment from the teacher. I knew that one plus one equaled two, but I couldn't write the numerals. Every moment was nerve-racking. I'm sure I was the last child at the bottom of the class.

Since I couldn't do the work, I started skipping school. I'd take my lunch pail into the cane field, and I'd knock some canes over so I could keep watch. When kids started leaving school for the day, I'd slip out of the field and walk home with them. Once I skipped school for an entire week.

But then the principal called Auntie Cynthia to ask why I'd missed so much. At dinner that night, Auntie Cynthia asked me about it. We all spoke patois, and what we said went something like this.

"How was school today, Yo?"

"Ok-k-kay."

"You stayed in class all day?"

I nodded and played with my food.

"You been going to school all week?"

"Y-y-yes ma'am."

She wrinkled up her face and shook her head. "You lie."

She got a switch and almost killed me that night, but she cured me of skipping school. So next, I got the bright idea that if I lost my reading book, the teacher wouldn't make me read anymore. That very morning, I threw my book in the fire pit outside the school. When the teacher called on me to read, I froze in my seat, then stammered that I'd lost my book.

My bright idea was not so brilliant after all. The teacher simply made me borrow a book, and when I gave my usual poor performance, she hit my hand. Later, someone cleaned out the fire pit and found my book partially burned. Unfortunately, my name was still visible on the inside flap, and when the teacher found out, she showed me the biggest belt I'd ever seen in my life. Burning a school book was a serious offense, and she must have kept that extra-wide belt for just such special occasions.

Why had I imagined I could outsmart the teacher? I just kept doing stupid things, and the more I failed, the more useless I felt. Our classroom had no clock. Instead, four bells divided each day, and the sound of that final bell was the sound of liberty. Thank goodness there was more to my life than school.

CHAPTER SIX

Prison And Freedom May Be The Same

My best friend was Audia, the younger of Auntie Cynthia's two daughters. She had buck teeth because she sucked her thumb and couldn't break the habit. She was also a tomboy, full of mischief. She loved to laugh, and she loved to eat sugar cane and mangoes. In fact, she loved all food.

Audia taught me how to make asham. We'd hollow out a bowl in the surface of an old tree stump, and then fill it with roasted corn kernels. Next we'd take a thick metal rod and pound the kernels into coarse meal. The final step was to add raw brown sugar, stir it up and eat it with a spoon. Corn meal and sugar, that's all there was to asham, but we loved how it tasted.

Whenever we could, we'd take off with a gang of cousins into the cane fields or up into the mountains. Uncle Man, my dad's closest brother, drove a bulldozer at the bauxite mine, and sometimes he'd give us rides in his bulldozer bucket. He'd lift us way up in the air, so we could see a long way.

Often in the cane fields, we'd find patches of marijuana. Ganja, we called it. People grew it for their own use, and there was a saying, "Ganja keeps away the cancer." We had a neighbor named Joe who was a Rastafarian, and sometimes, I'd smell ganja smoke coming out of his house. I never smoked it myself, but we didn't think twice about it. There were no drug runners or violence in those days.

Saturday nights were "movie nights" in Toll Gate. After sundown, a truck would pull up in the town center carrying a movie screen, and someone would set up a projector. The whole town would come out to watch. We'd sit on the ground or in lawn chairs. The movies were not first-run,but they were free. The first movie I ever remember seeing was *Rambo*.

Auntie Cynthia gave us chores, of course. Audia hated doing chores and complained about them constantly. For instance, our yard was bare ground, but we had to sweep the tree leaves and twigs that fell everywhere. We made our brooms out of palm fronds.

Audia said, "Why we have to clean this yard? It's just dirt."

I thought she made a good point. She tended to be defiant, and I often followed her example. By contrast, her older sister, Neshia, was "Miss Goodie Two Shoes" and did everything right.

Washing dishes was the worst chore. We did this every day, outside in the back yard on a zinc table under the palm trees. First we had to carry water from a communal pump about twenty yards from our house. Then we'd set up two water pots, one with soap suds and one to rinse. We used rags to scrub off the food stuck to the dishes. It was brutal. Many of my whippings came because the dishes weren't clean enough.

We also had to buff the concrete floors in our house each week with waxy red polish. Audia and I grumbled through the whole process. Since we didn't own an electric buffer, we used coconut hulls to spread the red cream. When it dried, we wiped and polished it with cloths. I remember bruising my knees buffing those floors, and if we missed a spot, guess what – we got a whipping.

Eventually, Audia, Neshia and I began working as a team to avoid whippings. Neshia was more feminine and proper. She rarely got into trouble, but Audia and I were always testing limits. I was neither a saint nor a delinquent. I just did what my cousins did, though I always seemed to have an excess of energy. Once my cousin Gareth put razor blades in the butter Uncle Dave fed to his cat. Gareth had heard that cats had nine lives, so he wanted to find out for himself. That time, I just stood by and watched, but another time, a bunch of us tied some cats in a burlap bag and threw them into a canal to see if they would live. An older cousin rescued the cats before they drowned, but Auntie Cynthia beat me for my part in that. With every whack, she said, "We'll see if you have nine lives."

Auntie Cynthia was strict, but she was there for me. Though I was not her child, she did her best to raise me, and I always felt that she meant well by me. She gave me tough love. She taught me how to tuck in my dress shirt and shine my shoes for church. She also laughed a lot, and she made me laugh, too. If I was good, she'd reward me by letting me watch "Tom and Jerry" and "The Pink Panther" on TV. Sometimes she'd cook special meals for me. My favorite breakfast was liver and fried dumplings. She and I are still in touch, and if she needs anything, I never hesitate to help her.

Maybe because Auntie Cynthia worked so hard, she seemed on edge, hurried and short-tempered. Audia and I were always into something. Me especially. I couldn't sit still or be quiet. I know I gave Auntie Cynthia trouble, but she was concerned and protective of us kids. She wanted to know where we were going and what we were doing. She warned us to stay away from the canals because we didn't know how to swim.

She'd say, "If you mess around that water, you'll mess around and drown."

Once that summer, we went to the beach on a church trip. Our whole congregation loaded up in an open-bed truck with wooden sides and a canvas roof. The truck took us into May Pen, where we caught the bus to the beach. Auntie Cynthia and the other ladies brought plenty of jerk chicken, bread, and Jamaican hot sauce for our lunch. We played on the beach for hours.

After lunch, we built a tower of people in the water, adults and kids together, twenty people kneeling on top of each other. I was small, so someone had to carry me to the tower because the water was over my head. I scrambled all the way to the top, and when the tower started to collapse, someone had to grab me because I couldn't swim.

But in the confusion, I slipped. When I fell into the deep water, I felt completely disoriented. The shaky underwater motion made me sick and dizzy, and I couldn't make sense of anything. I kept getting mouthfuls of water, and I panicked. Everyone was splashing, and I honestly thought I was going to die.

Finally Auntie Cynthia got me out, and I sat for a long time coughing, gasping and trembling. After that, I developed a fear of deep water. Only years later did I learn that the terrible disorientation I felt might have been due to a visual processing disorder related to dyslexia. People with this condition have trouble translating visual cues into estimates of distance and direction. This may be why so many people with dyslexia also develop motion-related phobias.

I couldn't blame dyslexia, though, for my fear of ghosts. Like everyone in Toll Gate, Auntie Cynthia was superstitious, and she taught us the local lore. Black cats were evil, and if you saw one, you had to be quick and close your eyes. If the cat passed on, everything would be okay, but if he lingered, you'd either have to kill him or die soon yourself.

She also warned us never to point at a grave or to use a curse anywhere near a grave. If you pointed at a gravestone, you had to bite all ten fingers. Otherwise, the "duppies" might come out and get you. "Duppy" was the Jamaican word for ghost, and when Auntie Cynthia was younger, she used to see them with her own eyes.

By custom, people in Toll Gate buried their loved ones in their own back yards, so my cousins and I could hardly run through the neighborhood without stepping on graves. During the day, we didn't worry, but at night, the graves scared me. Toll Gate had no street lamps, and very little light spilled from the houses, so darkness fell like a thick curtain. I knew all the paths through the bushes, and I could have walked them blindfold, yet I dreaded duppies.

When I finally saw one, though, it was broad daylight. The hot sun was beating down, and I was walking through the bushes toward my cousin Gareth's house, passing by a tombstone, when something made me stop. About two hundred yards away, across a field near an unfinished house, there was a big old tree we used to swing from. When I looked that way, I saw a figure in a white suit, and I thought, why in the world would that guy be wearing a suit, as hot as it is?

Then my heart jumped, and I dropped down behind the tombstone. When I raised up, the figure was looking in my direction. That's when I realized he wasn't quite solid. I could see through him.

Well, I bolted back to the house and wouldn't come out for the rest of the day. Later, I learn that Auntie Cynthia had a relative who'd been buried right on that spot, wearing a white suit. Man, that spooked me.

Those six months I spent in Jamaica, from March to August, 1990, come back to me now as half torment and half pure joy. The prison of school and the freedom of playing outdoors, I can't think of one without the other. For those two opposite reasons, that summer seemed to last forever, and I laid down a rich track of memories. But my parents had always intended for me to come back and start third grade in the States. So at the end of August, I packed my bags again.

CHAPTER SEVEN

If All Notes Were Alike, We Couldn't Have Music

While I was away in Jamaica, my parents moved from Teaneck to Cliffside Park, New Jersey. Cliffside Park was only six miles away from Teaneck, but much different, I realized when I flew back to the States in the fall of 1990.

Our new town stood on the banks of the Hudson River, directly across from Harlem. The streets were much more urban and noisy, with concrete everywhere, buildings crammed close together, and hardly any grass or trees. The apartment complex where we lived was more rundown than the one in Teaneck. And we didn't know anyone. Our neighbors were light-skinned immigrants, mostly Hispanic people. There were almost no black families. Worse, Kendra and Auntie Dahlia stayed in Teaneck, and we hardly saw them anymore.

Still, on the very first day, I met a neighbor who became my best friend. His name was Troy Corby, and he was a tall skinny white kid about four years older than me. While we were moving our stuff in, I saw him playing in his yard with his dog, Speck. Later when I went back outside, he was dribbling a basketball in his driveway.

He waved me over. "You wanna play basketball?"

He pointed toward the hoop mounted by his driveway. Then all at once, he started quivering. I mean his whole upper body shook. I didn't know it, but he was having a seizure. Then it passed off, and he acted like nothing had happened.

I'd never seen anyone do that before. I'd never played basketball either. But I said, "S-s-sure."

In time, Troy taught me not only basketball but also baseball, darts, skateboarding, and many other ways to have fun. He owned a super-cool BMX bicycle, and he bought pegs for the back wheel so I could stand up and ride behind him. Often his muscle spasms returned. I suppose he had a mild form of epilepsy, but he called the seizures his "tic."

The seizures never slowed him down, though. He and I played together for hours. I'd never owned a real toy, but Troy had everything. Sports equipment, video games, action figures. He had all the GI Joes and Ninja Turtles I'd ever wanted. Compared to us, Troy's family was rich.

Troy's father was not in his life. Troy lived with his mom and his older brother, Shaun, and sometimes I slept over in their house. They had the nicest family I'd ever been around. Troy had a cool room with bunk beds, and he and his mom loved to watch pay-per-view movies and wrestling on TV. His mom was a tall sweet woman with curly hair, and she made the best iced tea I'd ever tasted, never too sweet. I'd go to the kitchen to watch her make it. I remember she used Lipton powder from a jar. On Friday nights, she'd order pizza – an awesome treat!

Sometimes I wondered why Troy had befriended me, but now I understand that what we had in common was our difference. His tic, my stutter, we both knew what it felt like to be shut out and picked on. That was our bond. But Troy had a hot temper. He always needed to have his way, to win the games, to be right. Me, I could never keep my mouth shut, so we often got into arguments.

Troy's brother Shaun would yell, "You guys be quiet! I'm listening to music!"

Shaun was a relaxed sort of guy, but he loved his punk rock CDs. Troy preferred hard rock and heavy metal. His mom listened to country. In those days, I'd never heard of rap, but I knew all about punk rock, hard rock and country. My favorite band was Guns and Roses.

Troy had hairy arms and legs, and I could barely wait to grow hair on my legs, too, so I could be a man. During our years in Cliffside, my parents sent Michael and me to Jamaica each summer, and I remember the summer I came back with a fuzz of hair on my legs. The first thing I wanted to do was show Troy.

I'd never had a white best friend before. In fact, I'd never had a best friend of any color. Being around Troy and his family made me appreciate a different culture, and it helped prepare me to live in a wider world. Even now, I often think about Troy, and I've tried to find him. Someday I hope I will.

I didn't attend school with Troy because he was older, and I was just entering third grade. That first year in Cliffside, my parents enrolled me at P.S. 4, the local public elementary school. P.S. 4 had no playground, no grass, just concrete. It was a huge boxy building, four or five stories high, built in the institutional style with a wide staircase out front. I often got lost trying to find my classrooms.

My math teacher at Cliffside took a dislike to me almost from day one. Maybe it was because of my stutter. Or my poor performance. Or my restless inattention. Or maybe it was because I was the only black kid in the class.

She reminded me of one of the "Golden Girls" on TV. She had gray hair and wore frumpy clothes, thick black shoes and glasses. When I said "Hi" to her in the hall, she'd scowl at me and wouldn't answer. But if I said nothing, she'd say, "Excuse me? Hello?"

She seemed to take pleasure in calling me to the blackboard and making me do arithmetic problems when she knew very well that I couldn't. The chalk lines on the board might as well have been hieroglyphics. When my classmates laughed, she just let them. She never stuck up for me. She was mean to all the kids, especially the boys, but she just rode me. Once, I walked up to her desk to ask about a problem we were supposed to work, but I might as well have saved the steps. She seemed annoyed that I was bothering her, and the answer she gave was so short, I couldn't make sense of it. Then she ordered me back to my seat.

She told me I was operating on a kindergarten level, and to prove it, she made me look at the other kids' homework and test scores. "This is the work you should be doing," she said. But she never offered to help me. So as usual, I spaced out in her class and stopped trying.

However, I did make three good friends that first year in school, and we remained friends. The first was a little girl I'll call Sue Lin, the only Asian student in our class. The second was Jessica. She had bushy brown hair and a big smile, and she was a lot taller than any of the other girls. Last and best was Stacy Ann, whom I loved.

Stacy Ann wore glasses which magnified her soft blue eyes. She was small and thin, with a narrow face and long blond hair. Also, she had diabetes. She had to eat special food and take insulin shots, and kids often harassed her with questions, which made her cry.

In our various ways, the four of us were outsiders, and maybe that's what brought us together. We understood each other. While the other kids teased me for the way I talked, those girls acted as if my speech was normal. They were always nice to me, and I was crazy about them.

We ate lunch together and sat by each other in class. We talked a lot in school, which got us in trouble. Jessica lived near me, so she and I played together on weekends. Our school didn't have organized sports, but we played kickball and stickball in the street with neighborhood kids. I liked to jump gates, and I was a beast at kick-the-can. Stacy lived too far away to meet us on weekends, so I saw her only at school. She was the reason I stopped dreading Monday mornings. I even looked forward to school.

At lunchtime, Stacy always shared her snack with me. The school served good lunches, but I didn't have money to buy them. Every day, Mom made me a peanut-butter-and-jelly sandwich, and if I was lucky, she would toast it. If she was in a hurry, though, she'd tear the bread up with the cold peanut butter. I liked PBJ at first, even though Mom bought the crunchy kind, and I preferred the smooth kind. But after more than a year of the same thing every day, I started to hate it. So I really enjoyed sharing Stacy's snack.

She'd bring me turkey sandwiches or pizza-flavored "lunchables." That was sweet. Sue Lin brought sushi every day, fresh from the market, and she shared that with me, too. Sushi was fantastic.

One morning, Mom was making the usual crunchy PBJ sandwiches, and when she opened my backpack to stick my lunch inside, out tumbled two weeks' worth of moldy sandwiches. I had totally forgotten to throw them away. That goes to show how often I took out my school books.

"Whose backpack is this?" Mom demanded.

I said, "It's Michael's."

My little brother Michael also got PBJ for lunch, but Mike immediately said, "No, it's yours, Yo."

Mom turned to me and said, "What have you been eating for lunch?"

Against all common sense, I kept falling back on lies. "That's Mike's backpack. Not mine."

Michael shook his head and showed Mom his own backpack. I gave Mike a look then, as if to say, why did you tell her? You know how she beats me, and she doesn't do that to you.

But it was too late. She gave me a punch to my chest that rattled my head. Then she told Mike to bring the belt. She started throwing things and using vulgar language. It was bad. She kept beating me too long. Mike begged her to stop. When she finally wore out her anger, she made me pick up all the sandwiches and throw them in the trash. Then she warned me that Dad would give me another whipping that night.

He didn't though. When he came home, he asked me, "Why won't you eat your sandwiches?"

I told him the truth. I didn't think it was fair to have to eat the same thing day after day for months on end. I just couldn't eat PBJ anymore.

Dad listened. He didn't know I'd been getting the same lunch every day since second grade. I suppose he sympathized with me. He asked my little brother, and

Michael said the same thing. We were both sick of PBJ. So Dad told me that in future, he would do his best to give us a little extra money for school lunches. Also, after that day, Mom started sending us to school with Spaghetti-O's and Ramen noodles. I guess Dad had a talk with her.

Still, money continued to be a problem for our family. Dad's injuries from the fire often gave him pain, but his disability case had not yet been settled, so he continued to work with abused kids at the Center, and Mom continued to work multiple shifts as a nurse's aide. They both put in hard labor, although their wages were always low.

Since both parents were working, I walked to school alone, and for the first time, they gave me my own apartment key. At the age of nine, I became a "latch key kid." Michael was in day care, so every day after school, I spent hours on my own.

Sometimes, I would walk down to the banks of the Hudson River and stare across the water at Manhattan. The river formed a tidal basin at that point, so I watched the tides wash in and out. I didn't get too close, though, because the deep water spooked me.

Mom couldn't swim, but she wanted both her sons to learn for safety's sake. For a while, she took little Michael and me to swimming lessons once a week at the Red Cross, and I always dreaded it. Riding over in her Honda Accord, I'd start to get stomach cramps. That time in Jamaica when the tower of people collapsed and pulled me underwater still haunted me. I couldn't forget the horrible disorientation and terror.

The Red Cross instructor was patient, but I don't think she enjoyed putting up with my panic attacks every time I entered the pool. Even though I was the biggest kid in the swimming class, I had to wear water wings like a little child. I couldn't get across the pool without a float, and the other kids made fun of the way I talked. I wasn't learning, and finally we stopped going. Mom said it was a waste of money.

Around the same time, Jessica and I began playing flutophone together in the school choir. A flutophone is a wind instrument sort of like a recorder, except it's made of plastic, with simple finger holes for a child. I was a terrible player. I couldn't read the sheet music or remember the notes. Jessica tried to teach me, but I couldn't learn. Thank goodness the choir had a lot of flutophones, so I just hid in the crowd, moved my fingers around, and blew.

At Thanksgiving and Christmas, our choir visited hospitals and nursing homes to play for the old folks and the sick. Our choir leader would break us into teams of five, then each team would go to a different room and play. Those sick people touched my heart. I could read the suffering in their eyes, maybe because of what I'd been through myself. When they saw us coming, their faces brightened. Going with the choir on those trips made me feel good inside. That might have been where I first learned the importance of service.

But I couldn't hide in the crowd forever. One day, my turn came to stand up and play a solo. When the leader called my name, Jessica gave me a look that said, "This is going to be rough."

My hands were sweating when I climbed up onto the stage and stared at the music stand. As usual, the lines and notes floated off the page. So I put the flutophone to my lips and just blew. Out came a mishmash of squeaky notes, and the kids started giggling, even Jessica. Well, it was pretty funny.

"Jovan!" The leader's voice stopped me. "What are you doing?"

I gripped the flutophone and stared at my shoes. "I-I c-c-can't p-play."

"What have you been doing all this time?" she asked.

The back of my neck felt hot. I just kept staring at my shoes. Finally, she let me sit down, and Jessica got up to do her solo. After practice, the leader came and talked to me. I promised to work harder, and I guess she could see how much I wanted to stay in the choir because she gave me another chance.

From then on, Jessica started helping me before every practice. My goal was to learn one song, "Jingle Bells." I rehearsed for hours until I finally had all the finger moves memorized. That song made up my entire repertoire but, man, I could play it.

CHAPTER EIGHT

Warm Sun And Bitter Wind Each Have Their Turn

By spending our childhood summers in Jamaica, I was able to maintain my "green card" and permanent residency status. For me, each trip was a wish come true. The night before each trip, I would lay out all my clothes and think about the fruit trees, the sugar cane, and the blue mountains. I was too excited to sleep, imagining all the fun I would have. Next morning, Dad would drive Michael and me to the airport, and I would hold Mike's hand when we boarded the jet.

Once we landed, it was just like we'd never been away. Auntie Cynthia met us at the airport and took us to her house in Toll Gate. Audia and Neshia had a delicious snack ready for us, maybe fried dumplings. My older cousins grabbed me and wrestled and laughed. Right then, I knew that for the next few weeks, no one would call me a dummy or hit me because my report card was bad. Auntie Cynthia's house had no air conditioning, but I didn't worry about heat. I didn't miss Troy's pay-per-view movies or video games either. I had trees to climb!

Mike loved Jamaica as much as I did. He was just a little guy, and I looked after him, kept him out of the road, showed him the paths through the bushes, taught him to climb trees. One night in Auntie Cynthia's back yard, I was chopping wood with a machete just for fun, and Mike came over to watch. So I showed him how to hold the wood and chop at an angle, going with the grain. He wanted to try it, but I wouldn't give him the machete.

Next thing I knew, he'd found Auntie Cynthia's meat cleaver, and he was holding the wood flat, chopping it like a stalk of callaloo.

"Don't do it," I yelled, but right then, he chopped off the end of his finger. The tip and part of the fingernail were dangling by a shred of flesh, blood was running down his arm, and he was screaming.

"Auntie Cynthia!" I yelled. "Mike chopped his finger off!"

Everyone came running. Auntie Cynthia wrapped Mike's hand in a cloth. Then she called her uncle to drive them to the Mandeville Hospital. Watching them speed away in the old blue car, I couldn't stop crying. Mike was going to bleed to death, and it was my fault.

"He's g-g-gonna die," I told Neshia.

"No, he's not. Calm down. Come inside."

Neshia drew me a bath, and I sat in the tub, bawling my eyes out. I didn't know how to live without my brother. I felt certain the next time I saw him, he would be dead.

Five hours passed, the worst five hours of my childhood. I sat on the dark front porch, holding my head between my hands, waiting, dreading, and praying. After a while, I got in bed and hid under the covers. Finally, Audia came and got me. "They're back home," she said.

When the front door opened, Mike walked in smiling and showing off the big white bandage on his hand. He said, "They put my finger back on!"

For all the tears I had cried earlier, at that moment, I couldn't stop laughing.

Later on, Neshia told everybody what a baby I'd been. I tried to deny it, but Auntie Cynthia just smiled.

That summer in Jamaica seemed to last a lifetime, but flying home to Jersey, I began to feel I'd never been away. Knowing the whole cycle of school, grades and punishment was about to recommence, I felt the same miserable dread in the pit of my stomach. Sure enough, I had barely started fourth grade in Cliffside Park when my social studies teacher called my parents.

They told me later what she said. "Jovan has a learning disability." What surprised me was that this teacher actually

wanted to help. She urged my parents to get me a
speech therapist.

The teacher meant well, but I doubt if she could have
foreseen the consequences. Not long after her call, my
parents and I met with the school principal, and he agreed
something was not right with me. I had the lowest grades in
my class, and I was the only kid in the school who'd fallen
so far behind. Listening to him talk made me feel hopeless.

My first so-called "speech therapist" was a tutor provided
for free by the school system. He was a young college student,
and he met me four times a week after school. He did his
best as a tutor. He was patient and encouraging, but he had
no training in speech therapy. Our sessions lasted only three
weeks. In his final report to the principal, he said I was a good
kid who wanted to learn, but I was making no progress. He
admitted that he might not be the right person to help me.

When the free tutoring didn't work, the principal told my
parents I needed a professional speech therapist. This would
cost real money. At home, my parents often argued about
money, so I knew how little we had to spare. At least the
principal steered them to the Cliffside Park Early Learning
Center, which was more affordable for people like us.

The Early Learning Center reminded me of our school
library, one of my favorite places. The walls were decorated
with colorful posters, the shelves were full of educational
toys and games, and the sunny open rooms were always full
of kids. But I didn't like to sit still and pay attention. I wanted
play time.

My second speech therapist was a dark-haired man in his thirties who always wore a tie. I met with him every day after school, and he played memory games with me, using flash cards. I'd have to match a picture to a word, for instance "boat" or "cup." That had always given me trouble, so when I couldn't do it, he tried something simpler. He broke the words down into individual letters and had me write them. For me, though, the letters jumped around inside the words, so how could I remember what order they were supposed to come in? I kept getting distracted. I couldn't listen for long. At the end of our second week, he decided that he, too, might not be the right person to help me.

I overheard my mom talking to him on the phone, and every word confirmed that I was a really dumb child. That night I felt lost. I didn't want to be dumb. I had never thought much about my future, but I didn't want to go through life with no education. The next day, I sat on our front steps for hours, just thinking. Everything looked bad to me.

For the next several days, I was more spacey than ever. In school, I blocked everything out. I talked to myself. The teachers could not get my attention. Sometimes I daydreamed that I was a real Ninja warrior, as strong and swift as the action figures I played with at Troy's house.

My parents deserve a lot of credit for not giving up on me. They found a third speech therapist, a really expensive one this time. Mom's attitude was, "You get what you pay for." It still amazes me that they found the resources, and I don't know what they must have sacrificed.

My third therapist was a brunette lady in her early forties, and her office was in a downtown skyscraper. I couldn't get there on my own, so Mom and Dad rotated taking time off from work to drive me after school, then waiting till my session was over. The drive was twenty-five minutes each way.

The lady's office was nothing like the Early Learning Center. With its dull neutral colors and potted plants, it looked like a doctor's office. There were no other kids, and no games or toys on display. I felt nervous, but the lady was warm and encouraging. She had a corner office on one of the upper floors, with two glass walls looking out over the city. I'd never seen such a view.

On my first day, she gave me a test to determine what type of speech therapy I needed. I had to read words aloud. Then she would read words, and I was supposed to write them. The test revealed that my problem with language ran much deeper than just a stutter. Later she called my parents with her diagnosis: dyslexia, a serious case. This was the first time any of us had heard the word.

I saw that lady for twelve weekly sessions, which must have cost my parents a small fortune. She set a slow pace with me. Instead of launching right into the work, she would first make me feel comfortable, asking how my day was going. Then she'd explain what we would do that day. She'd ease me into it.

We played interactive games, like Connect Four where you take turns dropping colored discs into a grid and try to match four of the same color before your opponent does.

I enjoyed the strategy involved. I also enjoyed the jelly beans she kept in a jar on her desk, all except for the licorice ones.

When it came to matching pictures with words, though, I had the same problems as always. She spent three entire sessions trying to teach me to recognize Cat, Rat and Hat. She'd show me the word Cat, and I'd know it. She'd show me the picture, and of course I knew what a cat looked like. Then she'd flip the cards around and show them in a different order, and I could no longer recognize the word Cat. After a while, I preferred staring out her windows at the tall downtown buildings, and eating jelly beans.

In the end, she told my parents there was nothing she could do. "In all fairness," she said, "I just feel this is beyond me."

Driving home that night, my parents talked about all the money they'd poured down the drain for nothing. They didn't know where to turn next. At some point that year, they bought me a set of cassette tapes called "Hooked on Phonics," and over the next few weeks, both Dad and Mom tried to help me at home. Dad was more patient. My sessions with Mom usually turned into yelling fits. I had to constantly rewind the cassettes because I kept missing stuff, and the tapes soon stretched and got distorted. More money down the drain.

One Saturday night not long after that, Mom was in one of her moods, like a ticking time bomb. I was sitting in the closet to stay out of her way. The closet had no door, so I could see the television in the next room, and I was watching a wrestling match with Bret Hart, one of my favorites.

Mom said, "Yo, I need you to run to the 7-Eleven, get me some lettuce."

I was not happy to miss my show, but I got up, took her money and ran down the block to get the lettuce. When I got back, she opened the plastic sack. Something was wrong. She glared at me. I had seen that look before. Then she bunched up her lips and slapped me.

"This ain't no bleep bleep lettuce!"

I looked in the bag. I'd bought cabbage by mistake. I said, "Mommy, I t-t-thought it was l-l-lettuce."

She threw a pizza box at me, and when I retreated into the closet, she dragged me out by the arm. "Go back now and get me some lettuce!" Next thing I knew, she knocked my head through the sheetrock wall. "See what you did to the f—ing wall!" she shouted.

I grabbed the bag of cabbage and ran to the store, crying all the way. When the owner asked if I was all right, I couldn't answer. I sprinted straight back home. "H-here's the l-l-lettuce, Mommy."

She didn't say anything. When I went back into the closet, she turned off the TV.

My brother Mike had seen the whole thing, and he was crying, too. He came into the closet with me. "You okay?"

Mom scowled at Mike. "You want some, too?"

Mike said, "No, Mommy." Then we both just stayed in the closet.

When Dad got home, he saw the hole in the wall and asked me what happened.

"A-a-ask M-mommy."

"No, you tell me," he said.

So I told him. He just said "Okay," and walked off.

Even then, I knew Mom's whippings went too far. Jamaican parents believed in discipline, but there's a difference between discipline and abuse. A child with dyslexia and ADHD can stress any parent, but Mom whipped me as if she hated me. She disciplined Mike, too, but not in the same way, not with hate in her eyes. I used to get angry at Dad for allowing her to hit me so often and so hard. My parents had a lot of issues, and I guess Dad didn't want to start any more, but I still felt that he let me down.

The next day when I went to see Troy, his mom pulled me aside and looked at the bump on my head. Our apartment windows faced her house, and she told me she'd heard the whole thing. "Do you need me to call somebody?" she asked.

"N-n-no." I made her promise not to. I was too scared of what might happen.

Nowadays, I try to put these things into perspective. When my parents first left Jamaica, they must have dreamed of something better than our shabby, cramped apartment in Cliffside Park. Mom especially had been the first to venture out, seeking opportunity in the States. She'd married the strong handsome father of her child, but then he was crippled in a fire. Next, the son she'd had too early in life turned out to be lame in a different way. Maybe she felt the whole world was against her. Maybe that's why she seemed so full of rage.

Often I heard her yelling at Dad about the money they'd wasted on my speech therapy, and many times I saw that Dad's eyes were red. All the arguments were the same – money, Jovan, money, Jovan. She didn't tell me to my face, but I heard her say the words. "I just can't deal with a dumb son."

Not long after that, she packed up my little brother Mike, and the two of them took off to live with Mom's sister, Auntie Madge, in California. Cali, we called it, the land of opportunity.

I can't put into words how it felt when Mom walked out. Even now, I look for explanations, but nothing erases that wound. It's bad enough when strangers write you off, but when the person who's supposed to be in your corner disowns you, then nothing makes sense. Her rejection was worse than any blow from the belt.

Dad must have felt abandoned, too, though he told me she would come back. We led a quiet life after she left. No more screaming. No more punishment. But I missed my brother Mike. I felt bitter that she'd taken him away.

Things must not have worked out as she planned in Cali, because six months later, she did come back. What passed between her and my dad, I'll never know, but toward me, she seemed more resentful than ever. One thing was good, though. I had my brother again.

CHAPTER NINE

The Irony Of Lying Is That Lies May Come True

By the time I reached fifth grade, we'd moved into an even smaller, cheaper apartment in the same rundown complex in Cliffside Park. There were so many cockroaches, we had to set off an insecticide bomb. Mom was tense and moody. Anything might set her off. Almost every day, she nagged Dad about me. "What're we going to do with him?"

I'm glad she was more tolerant with Mike. She and Mike would roll around on the floor, laughing, hugging and wrestling. When she scolded Mike, he talked back to her, though I warned him not to. He was not afraid of her, and she didn't punish him. My strategy was to stay out of sight and keep my head down.

At school, my grades were bad, bad, bad, and every report card brought a beating. Often I went to school with welts on my face and neck. Once I had a split ear. After class one day, a teacher called me aside. "Are you okay?"

I just shrugged.

She said, "Every time I touch your shoulder, you flinch."

There was nothing I could say. I looked out the window.

She tried again. "Jovan, we can call somebody."

"N-no, p-p-please." I didn't want anyone to know. I thought my parents would kill me if I told anyone. Finally, the teacher let me go.

Stacy Ann was my confidante. I really had a crush on her. At school, she was the only bright spot for me, because every minute in the classroom felt like purgatory. Then one day in the library, she told me goodbye. She didn't want to, but her Dad had seen us together, and he ordered her not to talk to "that black boy." Her reason for breaking up kind of killed me. That was my first real encounter with racism.

If Mom and Dad had known about Stacy Ann, they might have separated us, too. "Stay with your own kind," they would've said. But I was crazy about Stacy Ann.

After that, I despised school. I wasn't learning anything, the teachers had given up on me, and my classmates treated me like a loser. Why put myself through the torture? So I started skipping school. I knew my parents' schedules, and for one two-week period, I didn't go to class at all.

Every morning I'd leave for school at the normal time, go around the corner, look at my watch, and wait till my parents drove away. As soon as their car disappeared, I'd run back upstairs and hang out in the apartment. At 2:00 pm, I'd go to the 7-Eleven, and if I had money, I'd drink a Slurpie, eat a hot dog and play video games. My favorites were Mortal Kombat and King of Fighters. When the owner asked why I wasn't in school, I told him I was sick.

Then one day, the worst thing happened. I left in the morning and did everything as usual, but then I broke my routine and went to the 7-Eleven early. Maybe I was extra hungry. I came back home and fell asleep. How was I to know my parents had that afternoon off?

I woke up hearing their key rattle in the lock. My bed was in the middle of the room right by the door, and I could see the door knob turn. My body felt like ice. I knew I was about to die.

In one desperate move, I bolted into the living room closet. Because it had no door, I scrunched in the corner and pulled some clothes down on top of me to hide. When they walked in, I prayed, "Oh Lord, please don't let them find me. Please make them leave."

But they didn't leave. No, they lay down on the living room couch to watch TV. An hour passed, and I sat dead still, trying not to breathe. My muscles cramped up. My head hurt. I thought, no way would I make it out alive.

At long last, they got up to go out, and Mom came to the closet to get her good shoes. Those shoes were lying right beside my foot. "Please, Lord," I silently prayed. I was shaking. But amazingly, she grabbed her shoes and didn't see me.

Dad left first. Then I heard the door close a second time, and the apartment sounded empty. I peeked out. No one was there. I went to the window and saw Mom's car pull away. In a flash, I raced full-speed back to the 7-Eleven to wait till school let out. I'd gotten away with it.

But not for long. My progress reports showed too many absences, and in time, the principal called my parents. Mom and Dad took turns grilling me, demanding to know the truth. When I broke down and confessed, Dad grabbed my shirt, and I thought he was going to punch me. So on the spot, I made up a story.

"There's a b-bully. A b-big white guy. He beats me up."

"Bully?" Dad frowned.

I started crying, selling the story. "He h-hurts me, Dad. I'm af-af-afraid of him."

Dad thought that over. "All right, we'll go talk to the principal."

That was the very last thing I wanted, but that's exactly what we did. My parents and I met in a small office with my teacher and the principal. My whole body was sweating.

"Who is this bully?" the principal asked.

"What's his name?" the teacher demanded.

I couldn't come up with a name. I'd made the guy up. When it became obvious that I was lying, Dad hauled me out to the car, threw me in the back seat and slammed the door. My Dad was a mild man. He had never laid hands on me. But that day, for the first time, he did.

Dad had an iron rule about lying. When we got home, he dragged me up to our fourth-floor apartment and flung me on the bed. Then he took off his belt and started flogging me. "You don't lie!" he yelled. "I'm not going to raise a liar!"

When I tried to cover up, he said, "Move your hand!"

Dad had served in the Jamaican Army, and I don't think he realized how strong he still was. The next day, I couldn't sit down properly. I had to perch on the edge of my chair in class. Why did I lie to my dad about a bully that didn't exist?

Not long afterward, a schoolmate was taunting me, and it was like a dam inside of me broke loose. This kid was no bully, just a smart-aleck. But I'd had enough. That day, I decided to fight back.

Here's how it happened. I was walking home from school with a bunch of neighbor kids, and this one Hispanic kid kept giving me a hard time. I'll call him Juan. He had light brown skin, and his nose was covered in blackheads. He was older and bigger than me, and he talked too much. For weeks, he'd been razzing me, making fun of my cheap clothes and asking why I didn't own a bicycle. Every day he took a shot, and usually I just let it be. But not that day.

I squared off and faced him. "I'm gonna f-f-fight you."

At first Juan just laughed, like he couldn't believe the tongue-tied Jamaican boy was finally speaking up. But when he realized I was serious, he stopped smiling. We arranged to meet the next day after school on a dead end street halfway between his home and mine.

Next day the word must have spread, because about fifty kids showed up to watch us fight. It was just like in a teenage movie. I felt nervous when I saw all those kids, but I'd made my decision. Juan was not going to insult me anymore.

When I walked up, he was dancing around, showing off for the kids, throwing air punches and bragging. I took off my backpack and laid it down. Then I moved in and hit him five times in a row. Next I picked him up and body-slammed him. After that, we heard police sirens, and everybody took off running.

I'd only gone a couple blocks when a police cruiser pulled up behind me. Something told me to stop. The officer got out, grabbed me and held me against his car while he called for backup. Another police car arrived. My heart was hammering. I was being arrested. They put me in the back seat of one of the cruisers and drove me to the police station, two blocks away.

They didn't handcuff me or put me in a cell. A man sat me down in an office and asked if I'd been fighting. I confessed everything, except Juan's name. In my halting stutter, I explained what had led up to it and how we'd

agreed to a time and place. Sweat was dripping off me.
I was too petrified to lie.

Next, the man made me wait while he called my
parents. Mom and Dad had to take time off from work to
come get me. Mom worked closer, so she arrived first. When
I saw her face, I wished the police had locked me in a cell.

She jerked my arm. "Why did you fight?"

"He was p-p-picking on me," I said.

"Did you beat him?"

I nodded.

She didn't say anything more to me then. She talked to
the police, and they let me go. They hadn't actually arrested
me. By the time Dad arrived, we were already back at our
apartment, and Mom was silent, like the calm before a
storm. Dad asked me what happened, and I told him the
whole story, the same as I'd told the police. Every minute,
I expected to feel the belt. But to my surprise, there was no
storm. Neither Mom nor Dad whipped me. I had defended
myself against a bigger boy, and they were proud of me.

Myself, though, I was not proud. I'd known all along
that Juan was just a loudmouth, not a real fighter. I never
doubted that I'd beat him. He lived down the street from
us, in a neat orderly home, with both his parents. He was
basically a good kid. In the weeks after that fight, Juan
and I became friends.

CHAPTER TEN

Guilt Stings Worse Than A Belt

That winter, Troy and I spent a lot of time together. He was sixteen, and I was just twelve, but I was tall for my age, already 5'8". We watched a lot of basketball on TV, and we played one-on-one in his driveway. When it snowed, we went sledding. Our next-door neighbor played high school football with the Cliffside Park Raiders, and Troy and I would talk to him when he came home from practice, still in his pads. He was a friendly Hispanic guy, and he told us he was hoping for a football scholarship so he could go to college. I'd never heard of football until then.

After that, whenever I walked to the 7-Eleven on Friday evenings, I started noticing the bright lights and crowd noises coming from the high school stadium. I wanted to see the Raiders play, but I never did. I got something even better. A friend of our family gave us three tickets to see the New York Jets play the Philadelphia Eagles at Meadowlands.

Dad took Uncle Woody and me, and as we climbed up to our seats, I just stared at everything. I'd never seen such an exciting and beautiful place as the Meadowlands football stadium. The green field as smooth as a carpet, painted with bright white lines and numbers, was surrounded on all sides by tiers of bleachers packed full of cheering fans. And shining down from above were the brightest lights in the world.

The stadium crackled with electricity. Wonderful aromas drifted on the air, hotdogs and sauerkraut, popcorn, French fries, nachos. When the teams came running out onto the field in their colorful uniforms, I got goose bumps. Then like everybody else, I jumped to my feet, clapped my hands, and hollered as loud as I could. I knew nothing about how football was played, and even after watching the whole game, I wasn't much wiser. But what a feeling, to be part of something that magnificent.

Later that winter, Troy's mom did me a truly kind favor. Her front yard had one of the few trees in our neighborhood, and Troy was building a tree house. He gave me a box of nails to hold, and as he hammered planks, I handed him the nails, one by one. It had snowed earlier, and when we ran out of planks, we took a break to go sledding.

My sled was an old inner-tube, which was hard to steer, and as I went sliding down the hill, I sailed off an ice-covered rock and fell six feet to the ground. That wasn't so bad, but then I noticed my left hand was burning. That box of nails was still in my coat pocket, and one of the nails had gone straight through the center of my palm.

Thank goodness the day was cold because my hand was almost numb. I walked back to Troy's house with that nail sticking out both sides of my palm, and all I felt was a little burning.

At first, Troy's mom wanted to call my mom, but I pleaded with her not to. I guess she understood my reasons by then. She pulled the nail out herself. It was new, not rusty. She poured some alcohol into the puncture, and that really burned. Then she dabbed on Neosporin and stuck a Band-Aid on each side of my hand. When I got home, I told Mom I had a little cut, and she never knew the difference.

Considering what a kindness Troy's mom had done for me, my next episode is hard to explain. It began one afternoon when Troy and I were in his room playing with his action figures. He'd just gotten the newest Ninja Turtle, the one with the red eye-mask and the two trident daggers. The one named Raphael.

It might sound strange that a twelve-year-old played with action figures, but I loved them, and so did Troy. Even today, I still collect them. While we lived in Jersey, Michael and I never owned any store-bought toys, but every kid we knew had action figures, and Troy had a bucketful. I craved them.

So I made my own. I got Toys R Us brochures and cut the pictures of my heroes out of the ads, then glued them onto cardboard to make them stiff. Every night, I marched them around and acted out brave adventures on the battlefield of my bedroom floor.

That day at Troy's house, though, I kept looking at his shiny new Ninja Turtle. Raphael was so perfect, so bright green, with that dashing red eye-mask, I wanted to keep him. I held him in my hands, made him fly through the air. When Troy wasn't looking, I slipped him into my coat pocket.

I knew it wasn't right, but I just wanted to keep Raphael for a little while. If I'd asked Troy, he would have said no. I held the turtle in my pocket and struggled over whether to give him back right then, but the temptation proved too strong. As soon as I got home, I hid Raphael under my bed. He was my secret treasure.

About three days later, Dad came home early. I'd been playing with Raphael, and he was still lying on my bed. Dad picked him up. "Where'd you get this?"

I ducked my head and stammered, "Troy let me b-borrow him."

Dad knew how protective Troy was of his toys, especially new ones. He gave me a suspicious look and said, "We'll see." Then he marched me next door to Troy's house.

When Troy's mom answered the door, I tried to get her attention. I kept silently shaking my head and pleading with my eyes, but she didn't get the message. Dad held out the Ninja Turtle. "Did Troy lend this to my son?"

"I don't recall," she said. "Let me ask Troy."

When Troy came to the door, he grabbed the turtle and said, "I've been looking for this."

Instantly, Dad knew I'd lied, and he did not put up with lying. He grabbed my shirt and almost lifted me off my feet.

Troy's mom got a worried look. She said, "It's no big deal. Just a toy."

"It's a very big deal," Dad said. "My son stole and lied."

Dad dragged me back up to our apartment and took off his belt. He hit me so hard, his belt split. With every lash, he said, "Don't steal. Don't lie." Mom stood in the doorway and kissed her teeth at me. That's a thing Jamaicans do, sucking air through the teeth to show disgust.

That was the second time in my life that Dad laid his hands on me. I knew I'd let him down, and that hurt more than his whipping. Still, I was glad the beating came from him and not from Mom. Hers would've lasted longer.

That afternoon, I went to tell Troy I was sorry, and my body was still shaking. He said, "Are you okay? We heard the whole thing through the window." Troy's mom even apologized for not covering for me. That made me feel even worse for what I'd done.

CHAPTER ELEVEN

I May Not Know My Purpose, But I Know The Game's Purpose

Finally in 1994, our family got some really good news. Dad's disability case was settled, and he started getting a benefit check every two weeks. Suddenly, money was not so tight, and Mom was all sunshine. She wanted us to move south to Florida, to be near another of her sisters, Auntie Dawn. Mom thought she could find a better job down there, and she and Dad started saving for a down-payment on a house.

We'd visited Auntie Dawn in Florida a couple times before, but that last year in Jersey, we went down several times, house hunting. Auntie Dawn and her husband Barry welcomed us. Her son Barrington was Mike's age, and we all got to be friends. They had a swimming pool in their back yard, and all the houses in their neighborhood had pretty lawns, flowers and shrubbery – the total opposite of Cliffside Park. Dad took Mike and me to Universal Studios,and I thought it was Disney World. I had a blast, though I was surprised not to see Mickey Mouse.

One event stands out in my mind from that trip. On our return flight, we were coming into the Newark airport in thick fog. I was looking out the window at solid clouds, thinking we were still miles high when, out of nowhere, the plane smacked the ground and bounced.

I screamed. I thought we'd crashed. A steward came running to see what was wrong, and it took me a long time to settle down. After that day, I've never felt the same about airplanes.

Still, I enjoyed visiting Florida. The hot sun and palm trees reminded me a little of Jamaica. The tropical colors and fragrances appealed to me, but at first, I didn't want to leave Cliffside. In spite of its faults, I'd figured out how to live there. I had friends. I had Troy. I didn't want to start all over. Nevertheless, in the summer of 1994, just after I turned twelve, we packed up everything we owned and moved to Fort Lauderdale.

My parents had found an affordable house in Lauderdale Lakes, in a subdivision called Oriole Estates. Though our house was modest by some standards, it was the nicest place we'd ever lived, with three bedrooms, a garage, a small back yard, and even a swimming pool. White brick with black mortar, the house was built in the shape of a U, with an orange tree out front. There were storm shutters in case of hurricane, and the lawn had its own sprinkler system. The American dream, at last.

We were all excited when we moved into our own home for the first time. Mom picked out new furniture, pictures, drapes and rugs at Wal-Mart. Everything had to match and be tasteful, and although I didn't like the kiddy stuff she chose for my bedroom – for instance, the comforter decorated in crayons – I absorbed her desire for style. Many years later in college, my Nigerian roommate Kelechi and I would have the most tastefully decorated room in our dorm.

Dad took pride in our home as well. He painted and did repairs. He kept the pool sparkling clean and the grass perfectly trimmed. Since he no longer worked at a job, he was always finding chores. Dad liked to stay busy.

Mom's creative outlet was sewing. She turned part of our new garage into a sewing room, where she made dresses for herself and her sisters, as well as church clothes for my brother and me. Inside the house, Mom was forever rearranging the furniture. It seemed like every Saturday, we'd move sofas or beds from one side of a room to the other. It was like she had a compulsion to control what little she could in her otherwise uncontrollable world. With a new mortgage to pay, she worked long weary hours, and even with Dad's bi-weekly checks, we were barely scraping by.

We loved our house, but the reason it was so affordable was its location. The fact was, we had moved into a ghetto. This was a new experience for me. In Teaneck, we had lived mostly around white people and Cliffside was mostly Hispanic. Lauderdale Lakes was all black. We were moving into the real 'hood.

Our subdivision was surrounded by pink and yellow project housing with graffiti on the walls and toddlers running around in nothing but diapers. Broken-down cars were permanent fixtures along the streets, and guys hung out at street corners smoking weed, probably selling it, too. Broken bottles littered the vacant lots, and concertina wire lined the fences. I often saw hypodermic needles in the gutters. Our local high school was known for violence, and police cars were always coming in to break up fights.

The kids in my neighborhood looked rugged. Some of them had dreadlocks and ornamental gold teeth, and they were edgy, hostile, always ready to take you on. More than once, I saw boys my age get jumped and beaten, and I soon learned which streets to avoid.

Nevertheless, something momentous happened to me that summer. Uncle Barry helped my brother and me sign up for Little League soccer and basketball. Uncle Barry was a coach at Tamarac Park, and Barrington played there, too. I'll always be grateful to Uncle Barry for signing us up and driving us to the ball practice and games. Those park leagues marked my introduction to organized team sports.

Of course I'd grown up around soccer – football, as it's known in Jamaica and the rest of the world. In Toll Gate, my cousins and I played the game in the churchyard, using big rocks to mark the goals. I'd also played street basketball with Troy in Jersey. But to actually have a coach, regular practices, uniforms, team mates – all this was new. I took to it like a bird to the air.

For the first time, I learned about player positions and game strategy. We played soccer on a real grass field with official goal boxes and painted boundary lines, and we played basketball on a real outdoor court. The excitement of competition thrilled me. In both games, I played defense, and I took pride in commanding my zone, not letting anyone score on me. Finally, I felt part of something bigger than me.

I never played offense. The only time I scored a soccer goal was by accident, when the ball bounced off my shin pad into my own goal box. In basketball, I could not make a lay-up or a free-throw, no matter how hard I tried. I was strong, fast and agile, one of the best athletes in the league, according to my coach, but even though I practiced for hours, my scoring skills never much improved.

Recent research has suggested that my problems with scoring goals were analogous to my problems with reading. Whenever I tried to read, the words on the page would start to float. Were the hoop and the goal box floating, too? Yes, they were. I was suffering from a visual processing disorder.

It's hard for me to explain the disorientation this caused me to feel. I've always had excellent 20/15 vision. I could see the goal just fine, no matter how far away, but I had to concentrate to pin down its exact location relative to myself. When I was dribbling or kicking a ball down the field, I had to focus all my attention on my footwork and the ball. I'd be hustling and moving like a champ, but if I looked up to locate the goal, I'd lose track of everything.

I was happy playing defense, though. The coach said, "This is what we need from you," and I accepted that. I liked being a defender. Sports brought a new and welcome structure to my days. Maybe I didn't understand my purpose in life, but I understood the game's purpose.

All in all, that first summer in Florida was wonderful. Not only did I find sports. I also made friends with a neighbor kid that everybody called T. I was sitting in my front yard when he stopped by to talk. He lived in our subdivision, and my dad had met his mom. T. was short and husky, with an afro and glasses. He wore clothes similar to mine – neither of us were up-to-date in fashion. T. was a gentle family-oriented kid, and I called him a "braniac" because he was very computer-savvy and had lots of video games. I liked going to his house. We played StarCraft for hours.

Also that summer, I taught myself to swim. We had a pool in our back yard, a deep worrisome well of water. Every time I had to walk by it, I felt the same sick fear I'd felt during the Red Cross swimming lessons back in Jersey. I imagined falling into that pool, losing all sense of direction, and never finding my way out. So it was self-defense that motivated my desire to learn.

At first, I stayed in the shallow end. I would hold onto the side and practice kicking my legs. Then I'd stand chest-deep and work my arms. Next I tried swimming, always close enough to grab the side. Many times, I scraped my hands and elbows because I swam too close to the side. When I gained enough confidence, I practiced jumping into the deep end with enough force to hit the bottom and kick back up. The instant I surfaced, I'd immediately lunge for the side.

My swimming got a little better, but still, I worried. I'd see Mom sitting by the deep end, dangling her legs in the water. Mom couldn't swim, and that made me anxious. What would I do if she fell in? I couldn't stand by and watch her drown.

My fears got tested soon enough, not with Mom, but with a cousin who was visiting us, a girl named Laura. She wasn't a good swimmer, so I kept an eye on her. All at once, she was splashing and struggling, four feet from the edge.

I swam to pull her out, but she was frantic. She clutched at me and pushed me under. When I tried to swim beneath and push her up, she started kicking me. I took a gulp of water. I saw the sun shining down through the surface, but how could I get there? It was just like back in Jamaica, when I was a little kid drowning in the ocean.

Then somehow my nose broke the surface, and I was thrashing. When I tried to breathe, water gushed into my lungs, but Mike was there. He used a long pole to pull me out, and I lay on the concrete gasping. He'd already pulled Laura out. Everybody was okay, thanks to Mike.

I lay by the pool at least twenty minutes, trying to catch my breath, and after that, I grew more determined to learn. Over the next few weeks, I gained enough skill to swim the entire length of the pool without holding onto anything.

I never tried this unless my parents were near, just in case. But eventually, I became a little more comfortable in the water.

CHAPTER TWELVE

Work Before You Play

Out of the blue, summer was over, and I entered sixth grade at Lauderdale Lakes Middle School. Kids start to grow up in middle school, and their agendas change. Even though the kids are still only twelve, thirteen, fourteen, they want to see themselves as independent and cool, like adults. But for me, that was just about impossible, not least because Mom picked out all my clothes at an open flea market called the Swap Shop.

Fashion was all-important in middle school, and it seemed that even kids from the projects had money for trendy styles. My clothes embarrassed me. Mom dressed me in loud, gaudy colors, and I had only ten outfits, which I had to rotate. I'd mix different shirts with different pants, but every other week I would have to start over again. Other kids never seemed to have to wear the same outfits. Also,

I had only one pair of shoes which I wore every single day, blue-and-white Converses with ugly black trim, not cool. One time, a girl asked why I constantly wore the same shoes, and all I could do was stammer.

On top of that, I got the "reduced lunch." Most kids brought money to buy their lunches, but my parents believed in saving wherever they could, so they applied for the "reduced lunch" program. Every day, they dropped me at school early for a 25-cent breakfast. Then at mid-day, I'd have to stand in a special line to get my 40-cent lunch. Everyone could see that I was poor, and for a growing boy, there was never enough to eat in the 40-cent lunch. Maybe a carton of milk, an apple and a burrito. That didn't fill me up.

The worst thing was my stutter, which made me scared to participate in class. In middle school, class participation counted toward your grade, but when I tried to speak in class, I felt the other kids giving me crazy looks. Every night, I prayed for my stutter to stop. If only that one thing would change, I thought my life would be better.

In our ghetto, it wasn't safe for me to walk to school, so my parents dropped me off every morning that first year. My school stood right across a fence from Boyd Anderson High School, the den of neighborhood gangs and fist fights, and the kids on that side looked like giants to me. Every morning, I'd go into the middle school cafeteria and get my meager breakfast, then come out and sit on the curb, waiting for classes to start. After one week of this, I totally went into a shell.

Most of the middle school kids knew each other. They'd grown up together, and their social cliques were already long established. So there I sat alone, the new kid, skinny and lanky with a thin neck, dressed in awful clothes, not a cent in my pocket and nothing to say for myself. What a dork.

I knew better than to try out for any ball teams at school. Whenever I saw the basketball players coming down the hall, I'd turn aside and move out of their way. They were popular, and they had each other's back. I was a nobody, with no one to back me up.

Class work was harder than ever, and my participation was terrible. If a teacher called on me to read aloud, I simply said, "No, trust me, I can't read." On multiple-choice tests, I marked random answers with barely a glance at the questions. The only class where I did well was gym, though I still kept to myself. Each day I ran the required laps, but when teams formed for any kind of game, I sat alone on the bench. The only time I worried about my grades was when I had to bring reports home and get signatures.

Monthly progress reports always came out on Fridays, and you can guess what those days were like for me. Yelling, whippings. I started waiting till Sunday night to show my grades, so I could enjoy the weekend and play my sports without fear. Sometimes I waited till Monday morning to get my report signed, when we were all in a rush to leave the house.

A few times, I asked my teachers to please give me better grades, but that got nowhere. Once or twice, I forged

Dad's signature, but my forgeries were too slow and shaky, so I got caught. With time and practice, my forgery skills improved, but it was easier just to alter the grades on my report. I used an erasable pen, and with one little mark, I could change every minus into a plus. I could also transform D's into B's. Sometimes, my teachers gave me looks when I handed the reports back in, but generally they let it slide.

Mom and Dad still tried to help me with homework, but when I couldn't grasp fairly basic things, they both grew impatient. They always worried about my grades, and Mom continued to punish me for not trying hard enough.

Sometimes I got a break in this routine when Mike and I spent weekends at Uncle Barrington's house. He lived in Lauderhill, a nicer part of town, and Auntie Dawn would order pizza or Chinese food when we came. Also, our cousin Barrington had a Sega Genesis console and lots of video games. Back then, I thought Barrington was a goofy kid. He laughed at things that I didn't think were funny, and he spoke very proper English. But there was not a bad bone in his body. He and I are still good friends. I loved going to their house – except for the times Uncle Barry gave us homework.

Why did he have to do that? I wondered. Wasn't the school week bad enough? He bought some educational booklets, ripped out some of the tests, and made us fill in the blanks. He'd sit in the kitchen with a timer and watch us while we worked, which only increased my stress. Afterward, he would grade our tests, and we needed at least 80 points to pass. If we failed, we couldn't go outside, and worse, we couldn't eat pizza. But Uncle Barry gave us two chances to pass.

I hated it. Even my parents didn't pressure me like that. Often, I failed and had to watch while the others ate pizza. You know, I really liked pizza. So I made a plan. Barrington was Mike's age, five years younger than me, but he always passed, so I started getting his help. He wouldn't take the test for me, but he would help me understand the questions. After that, I passed more often.

"Work before you play" was Uncle Barry's motto. Looking back, I see real magic in his words. That philosophy has paid off for Barrington. He recently graduated from Duke University, and now he's going on to medical school.

Uncle Barry was a manager at Walgreens. He was a small, light-skinned guy, hard-working, quiet and serious, and best of all, he didn't believe in violence. The punishments he and Auntie Dawn gave were time-outs or no TV, not whippings. Their home was different from ours, calmer and more affectionate. They showed me a different way for a family to live, and I wanted to grow up and be just like Uncle Barry.

Still, I didn't like school work. My best actual grade that entire first year of middle school was a C- in math on a weekly progress report. My final grades were dismal, and I still can't believe the teachers passed me on to seventh grade, but they did. That's where things began to change.

CHAPTER THIRTEEN

Friendship Is The Best Safety Net

When I turned thirteen, my parents decided to stop driving me to school, so beginning in seventh grade, I walked alone every day. Sometimes if Mom was in a hurry, she even trusted me to walk eight-year-old Michael to his elementary school.

But our 'hood was treacherous. In the streets, anything could happen, and you needed backup to be safe. People wouldn't touch you if they knew there would be payback from your cousins, your friends, or your gang. But if you were alone, like me, you were an easy target. So I tried to be invisible. Every day, I took the long route behind the grocery store because the shorter way past the high school was too risky. Still, I stayed keyed up the whole time, watching over my shoulder.

There was one particular corner which I could not avoid, where a guy named Big Chris hung out with a bunch of high school punks. Big Chris rarely went to school. I didn't know his age, but he was much larger than me, scary and mean-looking. The word was, he and his friends sometimes beat people up, so I made a point of passing him on the opposite side of the street.

Big Chris didn't know me, and I never did anything to draw his attention. But one day as I was walking home, he yelled across the street at me. "You! Hold up."

I kept my head down and walked faster, praying he'd let me pass. He had no special reason to jump me. But when he clenched his fists and started coming across the street, I dropped my backpack and ran.

He and his friends chased me for about a block, yelling insults and laughing, but I sprinted lightning fast, so they soon gave up. When I finally stopped, my heart was thundering. Somewhere behind lay my backpack with all my textbooks inside, but I didn't dare go back.

When I got home, I told Mom that someone had stolen my backpack at school. Considering the reputation of my school, she must have found that story easy to believe. She didn't hit me, and in time, she took me to the Swap Shop to get another JanSport backpack. Thankfully, the school replaced my books.

But that wasn't the last I heard from Big Chris. A week or so later, I came home to find him sitting in our front yard, talking to my dad. I stopped still, not sure what to do. Maybe he hadn't seen me. The way he talked to my dad, he was like a different person, super polite.

When I entered the yard, Dad said, "Chris, this is my son, Jovan."

Chris and I just nodded at each other. We didn't say a word, and I hurried into the house. Later, Dad told me that Chris often stopped by for a talk, and they'd become friends.

The next time I saw Big Chris on his corner, he called out, "Jovan! What's up?" Then he motioned me over in a friendly way. This time, he didn't seem threatening, so I stepped closer.

"I didn't know you were Mr. Haye's son," he said. "Let me know if you have trouble with any kids. I'll deal with it, okay?"

From then on, Big Chris and I were cool. I could pass his corner, no problem. That episode made me realize people are rarely who they seem just from the outside. Every person has another story, and we'll never know all the reasons why people are who they are.

All that summer, I'd been playing Little League soccer and basketball, and my skills had steadily increased. As the season ended, our soccer team won the League Championship, and I was named Best Defensive Player of the League. That same year, my "Crazy Legs" brother won Best Offensive Player in his age group.

So when autumn came and school started, I began to join in the ball games in gym class, instead of sitting alone on the bench. Now that I understood how to play, I enjoyed it. I actually looked forward to gym. Our middle school basketball team was called the Vikings, and every morning before class, the players would practice throwing and catching. I knew some of them from Little League, and after a while, they let me join in. My P.E. teacher was also the team coach, and he must have been watching, because he told me to try out for basketball.

I loved basketball, but I thought the guys who played football were the coolest. I saw them walking around in their team jerseys, talking about their games. They were the "big men," and I wanted to be one of them. But my parents wouldn't allow me to play football. So when the coach suggested basketball, I went for it.

The Vikings had a lot of good players, and school teams weren't like the "recreational" leagues at the park. You couldn't just sign up to play. You had to prove your worth. Man, I was nervous on try-out day. All of the other guys who were trying out knew each other, and many of them were bigger and more muscular than me. But what I recall as the worst thing about that day was having to wear the same old blue-and-white Converse shoes that I wore to school every day of the week.

Despite everything, I made it. I hustled like crazy and made the team. A couple of weeks later when our uniforms came in, I got two new pairs of game shoes and one pair of practice shoes. I was in.

Once I made the basketball team, everything became more "chill," as we kids used to say. I wasn't alone any more. I had teammates at my back. From then on, I could take the shorter route past the high school without worry. Oh, I still didn't walk around school with my chest out or hang with the cheerleaders like the other guys did. But I felt more relaxed. A guy named Abdul Hodge played on our team, and he had brothers in high school. When he and I got to be friends, that gave me even more security.

At one point, somebody on our team got jumped, and the next day, about thirty guys were waiting to get even. After that, nobody bothered our team again. I'd go with my teammates to a nearby convenience store, grab something to eat and hang out, talking. That never could've happened before basketball. If I went to watch a high school game, as long as I saw one of my teammates there, I felt safe.

Of course, the best times were on the court, and I could barely wait for practice every day after school. We had a strong team, and I felt terrific just being able to play with such excellent athletes. I was one of the "role" guys, meaning I did what the team needed me to do. I played Power Forward, but I didn't worry about shooting goals. I let the other guys make the flashy moves, catch the rebounds and make the scores. I was there to hustle and move our team down the court.

If we had a big game coming, I could hardly focus on anything but practice. Friday couldn't come fast enough. On game days, I wore my jersey to school instead of the same old outfits from the Swap Shop. And then Friday night came, and it was game time.

I still remember the excitement of those Friday nights. Our school band played, and lots of people showed up to cheer. In south Florida, basketball and football were BIG, and people took pride even in middle school teams. The competition was fierce. We'd be out on the court, moving in sync, hearing the fans roar. More often than not, we'd win. Then our whole team would celebrate together. There's no better feeling than the happy exhaustion after you've exerted your best effort, the sense of being part of something bigger, the pure love of the game.

Basketball taught me some solid lessons about teamwork, dedication, hard effort and focus on the goal. Some of the relationships I formed with my middle school teammates have lasted through college and even to the present day. Still, it's probably true that my intense involvement with sports interfered with my homework time.

I would come home tired after practice, about 7:00 pm, and all I wanted was to eat supper and rest. The last thing on my mind was homework, because in middle school, kids could stay on the team regardless of grades. Of course, my parents still pressured me to do better, and Mom still punished me on report card day. But I think they were both pleased to see me playing ball, learning to fit in, finally doing something well.

For my entire first year in Florida, I'd been shell-shocked, but after I made the basketball team, I actually started doing better in academics. Not great, but better. For one thing, my stutter was fading. My prayer had finally been answered, and I began to speak a little more clearly. From the research I've done, I now know that many children who stutter at a very early age grow out of it around puberty. Once my stutter faded, I was more willing to participate in class.

My report cards still showed low grades, but there were many Incompletes, and I learned a lot about the letter "I." Incomplete meant a second chance. So I did extra credit work and took tests over whenever I could to improve my grades.

When my teachers saw I was trying, some of them stayed after class and gave me one-on-one instruction. I really appreciated that. Without the other kids around to judge and make me nervous, I comprehended more. Once, when a teacher had to cancel a session with me, I felt real disappointment. I'd actually been looking forward to our lesson.

At home, Mom's regular whippings didn't bother me as much. I'd gotten tough-skinned, and wiser. Mostly, I stayed in my room, out of sight, invisible. Michael was different, though. He liked to spend time with Mom and Dad. He was outspoken, full of energy.

I used to warn him not to act so lovey-dovey around Mom, and especially, not to talk back to her, because I knew how unpredictable she could be. I didn't want to see Mike hurt, but he never listened. The truth was, he and Mom were genuinely fond of each other. Well, he was an easy kid to like.

Often, my parents threw parties in our house for friends and family. They played music, and Mike loved to dance. Though he didn't know a step, he'd gyrate around like a wild boy, and he'd always be laughing. He liked people and commotion. Not me, though. When Mom tried to make me dance, I felt awkward, and I hated it. I preferred to hang out with the little kids in my room where it was quiet.

But as Mike grew older and saw more, he did me generous favors. Mom never hit Mike as hard as she hit me, so sometimes he took the blame for my transgressions. Once when Mom found an empty juice box I'd put in the fridge, Mike said he did it. Another time, I'd just had a major beating and my bruises were still sore, so Mike stepped in to take the next beating for me. My bond with Mike has always been stronger than the bond with my parents, and I thank the Lord for giving me such a brother.

Still, he was lazy growing up, and something of a smart-aleck. If it was his turn to wash the car, he'd ask, "Why do I have to wash it? I can't drive it." Mom might tell him to wash dishes, and he'd say, "I didn't use them." One night, to show out, he washed only his own plate, cup and fork.

I would never say or do such a thing. I actually liked to help clean up around the house. Mike's risky behavior worried me, but he got away with a lot. I looked out for him, of course. Me, the protective big brother. I took him to the park, and if I had money, I'd buy him toys. I shared my food with him. I'd speak up for him when he had to show a bad report card to Dad. One day I even saved his life, as he had once saved mine that time in the swimming pool.

It all began when Mom bought us some food at MacDonald's, then dropped us at the house while she ran errands. By the time we sat down to eat, my cheeseburgers and his Happy Meal were cold and dried out. I microwaved mine, but Mike couldn't wait. He stuffed his mouth full of cold, hard French fries.

Next thing, he started coughing, then gagging. Then he put his hand to his throat, and no sound came out at all.

We were alone in the house. I yelled, but no one could hear. The Heimlich maneuver was something I'd heard of, but I didn't know how to do it. At first, I slapped Mike on the back, but that didn't help. His lips were turning blue. So I rag-tossed him. I threw him up in the air, and he landed on his back. Then I jammed my fist into his upper abdomen. I gave him six or seven good pumps, and all at once, the fries came up.

After a minute, I gave him some water to drink, and he was okay. We didn't tell anyone about that. It was our secret.

CHAPTER FOURTEEN

Miracles Come In All Sizes

All through middle school, I still felt a constant urge to talk, and often I talked to myself. But if I liked a girl, I couldn't open my mouth. Girls talked to the popular guys, and I was not in that category. I still had to stand in line for the "reduced lunch." Plus, my clothing was a serious drawback. All the cool guys wore "Starter" jackets, made by the Starter Clothing Line. Each jacket carried a college or pro team's colors and logos, and they were a huge status symbol in those days. Me, I still wore outfits my Mom picked out at the Swap Shop. So I stayed away from social life. I remained a home body.

By eighth grade, though, I'd become a key player on our basketball team. My coach often praised my abilities, but he said that in order to play in high school, I would need a certain grade point average. Man, that was bad news for me. I couldn't bear the thought of giving up the game, so I began to put more effort into homework.

One day, my English teacher was helping me work through a lesson, and after a while, she said, "Jovan, have you always struggled with English?"

"Yes ma'am," I told her. "They say I have dyslexia."

She nodded. "I kind of figured that."

We got into a discussion, and I told her about the speech therapy I'd been through and how little it had helped.

"But when you try, you do better," she said, to encourage me.

Sure enough, the more I tried, the more all of my teachers responded with offers of help and extra credit work. In my final year of middle school, instead of D's and F's, I started getting more C-'s. For me, that was like an A+.

Finally, I stood in line in the middle school gym, wearing my maroon-and-gold cap and gown, while Mike and my parents waved from the audience. Middle school was over. My next stop would be that den of drugs, brawls, knife fights and gangs – high school.

Boyd Anderson High School was overcrowded, underfunded and violent. Its academic record was dismal, and its hard-pressed teachers would not be able to offer much help to a shy boy with dyslexia. I dreaded going there, but it was my neighborhood school, so I had little choice.

Then a miracle occurred. Some of my coaches from the Little League teams also coached at a magnet high school called Dillard, and they encouraged me to apply. Maybe they wanted my athletic skills on their school teams. My grades had gotten somewhat better, but I didn't have much hope of being accepted.

All through the final weeks of summer, I said my prayers and waited to hear. Boyd Anderson loomed like a bottomless pit. Then one Saturday afternoon, the letter arrived in our mail box. I was so nervous that I couldn't bring myself to open the envelope.

Dad was sitting in the open door of our garage, watching TV. He saw me standing by the mail box, staring at the envelope in my hand. "What've you got there?" he said.

I took a breath and tore the envelope open. I couldn't read the letter. I don't think I ever did read it in full. My eyes went straight to the bold words at the top. "You have been accepted."

I let out a whoop so loud that everybody on the block must have heard me. Dad came over, took the letter from my hand and read it. I was dancing around, so relieved, so happy.

Then I saw a big smile on Dad's face. "Ah man, good job!"

Mom came out of the house, and when she saw the letter, she was happy, too. "But you know you've got to bring your grades up," she said.

"I'll do my best," I told her.

"Bring up those grades. That's your job," she said again.

By that point, I was growing taller. My clothes fit tighter, and my shoes pinched, so in the final days before class, Mom took me shopping. I couldn't tell her that I preferred to shop on my own. The way she picked out my clothes and checked the fit of my jeans in public embarrassed me, but I couldn't say anything because I didn't want to get "the speech."

She took me to the Swap Shop, and for the first time, she also took me to a place called Tempo in the Lauderdale Lakes Mall, a place where the older teens went to shop. She bought me a new JanSport backpack, plus three pairs of shoes and enough outfits to last two weeks. I guess she realized that in a magnet high school, I would need more. I wanted the Patrick Ewing shoes because Ewing was a Hall of Fame basketball player from Jamaica, and his shoes were the coolest. But we couldn't afford them, so I got two pairs of last year's edition Nikes and one pair of Reeboks – way better than the old Converses I'd had before.

Dillard High School was about fifteen miles away, in Sunrise, Florida. On the first morning, Mom dropped me off out front, and that was the first time I saw the place. Dillard was like a mini college campus, with three buildings and a lawn with trees and green grass. The buildings were clean and modern, really nice. I asked my way to the front office to get my schedule, and as I was crossing the lawn, I saw students with dreadlocks, baggy pants and gold-capped teeth. Some of the girls were dressed like they were going out to a club. They looked just like the ghetto kids at Boyd Anderson.

Though Dillard was a magnet school, it was still situated in the 'hood. All around were the usual low-budget homes and housing projects, and plenty of local ghetto kids went to Dillard. But as I kept walking, I saw a separate group of kids wearing more conservative clothes. There was a well groomed Asian guy in glasses, a Muslim girl in a head scarf, and several white kids. As soon as I entered my first classroom, I realized these were the magnet kids.

That same day, I learned the magnet program had its own building, and though we sometimes took classes with the local kids, the magnet kids stuck together. We always knew who was who, and no one messed with us. Our side of campus was calm and studious, while on the other side, fights often broke out.

The school had a problem with theft, and when we dressed for P.E., I had to keep my backpack with me, because the lockers had no locks. Experiences like that made it hard for me to trust anyone. Even now, I often feel for my wallet. It's one of my many small compulsions.

For the entire first semester, Mom continued to drop me off, and I always arrived late because Mom had a habit of rushing out at the last minute, and she had to drop Mike at his school before she dropped me. Arriving late meant I had to go to In-School detention, so I missed my entire first-period class.

In second semester, I started riding the school bus. Although I had to get up earlier, the bus was more reliable and also more peaceful, because Mom couldn't lecture me about how to carry out my day. On the bus, I could sleep or do homework, and I didn't have to miss my class.

That first year at Dillard, I went out for junior varsity basketball, and I made the team. Coach "Rock" Nelson was as hard-driving as a drill sergeant. If there was a dictionary for profanity, he would have written it. The first time I heard that kind of language coming from a coach, I was shocked. He had a strong team of players, though. Some of the guys were 6'9" or 6'10". Compared to them, I was pretty short at 5'11", but I was rough and tough, very competitive. Still, for a guy my size, going against players over six feet tall was a challenge.

Early on, Coach told me that basketball would not be my game. He said, "Son, you don't have the height for it. If you want a scholarship to college, football's your best chance. In football, you can make something of yourself and help your parents, too."

Believe me, I wanted to try out for football. College seemed like a distant dream, but football was real. The NFL games on TV made me yearn to be part of it. In high school, everybody talked football. On Friday game days, the players walked around in their team jerseys and flip-flops, looking magnificent, and we'd hear the band practicing. Basketball games were important, but you could feel the football buzz in your bones. After school, we'd see the team boarding a line of school buses, and I dreamed that I was one of them.

I didn't have transportation to go to our football games at Lockhart Stadium, but I often watched our guys practicing after school, all decked out in their pads, helmets and hardware. I felt sure that if I got out on the field with them, my talent would show. But my parents refused permission. They pointed out that most football players started in sixth grade, whereas I had never played a single organized game. They didn't think I'd be able to catch up. Plus, they worried that I might get hurt.

Their doubts gave me second thoughts, too. Dillard had a powerhouse football team. The players were huge, and their size intimidated me. I had not yet reached my full height or weight. Plus, the players all knew each other, and none of them knew me. Only six magnet students played junior varsity football, and I'd just met them. So it was basketball for me.

Coach Rock pushed us hard. He didn't believe in losing. Our team was named the Dillard Panthers, and he had what he called "Panther Periods," two hours of brutal conditioning. First we'd run fast laps. Then we'd do "suicide" drills, running back and forth from the base line to half court, then back to the free-throw line, constantly turning and pivoting. Next we'd run the stairs. Some of the guys puked or passed out during "Panther Periods." I lost my lunch a few times, too.

Coming from middle school to this team was a shocker. Coach Rock scared me. He saw right away that I couldn't score, but he loved how I hustled on defense. The guys nicknamed me "Jungle," because they said I played like a wild jungle animal. Coach made me Power Forward, and once again, I accepted my role. In fact, I found defense more satisfying, diving for the ball, blocking shots, imposing my will. Defense required more energy, and I liked that.

Dad and Mike came to all our home games. Our team was strong, but if we lost, Coach gave us a "Panther Period" the next day. Twice after losing on our home court, Coach was so mad, he gave us a "Panther Period" that same night. Those work-outs were killers. And no matter how hard I tried, I never developed the knack for shooting baskets. If someone fouled me and I had to make a free-throw, Dad would just cover his eyes.

A free-throw is a rhythm shot. I learned that from studying the great players on TV. I analyzed how they made the same exact moves every time. Their shots were as graceful as a perfect golf swing. Me, I came up with a dozen different techniques, none of which worked. At that time, it didn't occur to me that my difficulty might be related to dyslexia. In addition to the way my visual processing disorder affected my ability to locate soccer and basketball goals, another dyslexia-related condition called "dysgraphia" interfered with my ability to carry out repetitive sequences, like free-throws.

At one practice, Coach was running late, so he gave us what he called a "quick shoot-around." He said, "As soon as everyone makes two free-throws in a row, you can all go home."

Coach stressed free-throw skills as part of our game strategy, and he made us practice them a lot, so even players with low game skills could make free-throws. I got in line and watched the guys ahead of me. Miss, miss, score, score. The line moved quickly.

My palms were sweating when I stepped up for my turn. By this time, all the guys were eager to go home. I stared at the basket. I could see every detail of the metal hoop, the net, the backboard. But its exact location in space eluded me.

I made my throw. Miss. Miss. After six misses in a row, I could hear the guys getting restless. Coach said, "This is a real f—king shame, kid. You gotta do better."

After twelve misses, my teammates were grumbling, and I was crying inside. No one could go home till I finished. I was letting my team down. Finally on the thirteenth try, my ball sank through the net. But then I had to get a second goal in a row.

One hour and forty minutes later, I finally made two straight goals. When my final shot bounced off the backboard and tipped into the net, everybody in the gym shouted, "Thank God!" I wanted to melt into the floor. For the rest of the day, I didn't do anything.

After that experience, Coach still started me as Power Forward in every game, but he usually took me out toward the end, to avoid the risk of someone fouling me. Each time I saw my dad drop his head, I felt miserable. Nevertheless, I gave the game my all, and eventually, Coach said I was one of the best basketball players in junior varsity.

CHAPTER FIFTEEN

Let Go Of Your Crutch

Freshman year at Dillard High School was rough, and though I excelled on the basketball court, I continued to lag in academics. The classes were much harder, and we had only ten minutes between bells, so we had to hurry across campus, fighting crowds of other kids. As before, basketball practice kept me late after school every day, and when I got home, I had little energy left for homework. Though I comprehended what kids read aloud in class, reading the text on my own was still an ordeal. That meant I gained only a partial grasp of each subject, and there were times when I felt really discouraged. Every day I prayed, "Lord, please just let something good come out of this high school."

He answered. I made a good friend that year. Nigel Seaman came from Dominica, a Caribbean island near Martinique, and like mine, his parents were strict. Nigel and I were both large, quiet, athletic kids, and we got along well. He had short wavy hair and glasses, and he was very bright. He took a lot of difficult classes, and he always made honor roll. He and I had computer lab together.

I fell behind Nigel in academics, though, and it shames me to admit that, on the first few tests of my freshman year, I cheated to get a passing grade. Good grades were required to keep playing basketball, and any test with a time limit made me panic. I had to read every question over and over to understand it, and sometimes I'd spend eight minutes on just one question. So I stole peeks at the smart kids' papers and copied their answers.

My biology teacher was Mrs. Knight, a Jamaican like me, and she caught me cheating twice. I denied it, but she knew, and she gave me an F both times. She could've reported me to the principal if she'd wanted. Mrs. Knight was every bit as demanding as the teachers in Toll Gate. She didn't tolerate poor work. She was a short, dark, soft-spoken woman, and when she got excited, her strong Jamaican accent would come out.

Because of our shared background, Mrs. Knight took a special interest in me. She made a point of calling on me in class and pointing out my errors. She called my parents about my learning problems. Once or twice, she kicked me out of class for talking. She stayed on me, just like an auntie, insisting I could do better. I didn't like her attention at first, but she was right. She encouraged me to believe in myself.

Another teacher made an enormous difference in my life that year. My English teacher, Mrs. Patton, was a middle-aged white lady with curly light-brown hair and glasses, very sweet tempered. I never heard her raise her voice, and sometimes when the other kids treated her rudely, I felt bad for her. She used to say, "I'll do my best to teach, but learning is up to you."

Frankly, I didn't give my best in her class at first. I still found it difficult to focus on topics that held no interest for me. Often, I came to school tired from basketball practice, and sometimes I fell asleep during her lectures. If I wasn't sleeping, I was talking. I couldn't go twenty minutes without talking. Even now, I feel a constant urge to talk, and if no one's around, I talk to myself.

But one day, Mrs. Patton assigned us a research project on the history of the English language. We were allowed to choose any aspect of the topic, so I did my research on the history of Jamaican patois. For once, the research really engaged me, and when I had to stand before the class and present my findings, I felt natural and easy. Usually, I disliked public speaking, but this time was different. I had something to say that I cared about.

A few days later, Mrs. Patton called on me to read a paragraph aloud and explain its meaning. The text had a lot of unfamiliar words, and I knew it would not go well, so I refused. After class, she held me for a talk. We sat down together, and I saw my file open on her desk.

"You have dyslexia," she said.

I nodded. "Yes ma'am."

Then she gave me a direct look. "Jovan, there are some in this class who want to learn, but your constant talking distracts them."

I hung my head. "Yes ma'am."

"I understand you've had a hard time," she went on, "but you have to stop using dyslexia as a crutch. I know you can do well when you try. You've shown me that."

Those words made me lift my head.

She looked me right in the eye. "Dyslexia is not holding you back. It's your own lack of commitment."

What she said went through me like a cold blade, because in that moment, I knew she was speaking the truth. My body shook. My hands sweated. I'd been using dyslexia as a crutch.

She kept talking. "When you exert yourself and put forth the effort, you're as capable as any straight-A student in this school. Jovan, I will not let you pass my class without trying."

"But what if – "

"Stop." She put up her hand. "Don't say anything. Just think it over. Now, go on to your next class."

She wrote me a pass so I wouldn't get in trouble, but in the next class and for the rest of that day, I couldn't pay attention to anything. Even basketball practice was a blur.

All I could do was think about her words. She'd called me out. She'd forced me to see I'd been lazy. I had to let go of dyslexia. I had to beat it.

That night, I lay on my back in bed staring at the ceiling, and I prayed again. "Lord, help me get through this." Tears ran down my face. "I promise I'll do better, Lord. Please help me."

He must have heard, because suddenly, a light switched on. For the first time in my life, I believed in my heart that I could fight and defeat dyslexia. No one could do it for me. My school didn't offer help for special needs like mine, but speech therapy wasn't what I needed. I needed to commit. I needed to study harder and prepare ahead more. My learning process was slower, but equal to the task. Suddenly, I knew I could do it.

To this day, I thank Mrs. Patton for kick-starting me. After she talked to me, I made up my mind to stay focused in class. I stopped talking. I never let myself fall asleep. I vowed never to cheat again. I also stayed up late at night to do my homework.

It's not as if a miraculous transformation occurred. The changes took time. After a while, I learned how to squeeze extra work into every spare minute, even during the day at school. On weekends, I did homework first thing on Saturday morning instead of waiting till Sunday night.

To improve my reading skills, I developed several helpful techniques. First, I simply followed along in the text while others were reading aloud. I would run my finger along the lines and point at each individual word to keep my focus. Sometimes I used a straight-edge or a folded piece of paper to keep the lines of text from waving around. That helped a lot.

Next, I taught myself to skim sentences quickly and pick up the meaning without reading every word. I also spent much more time preparing before class. Alone in my room, I practiced reading aloud, and if certain words gave me trouble, I underlined them and worked harder to understand and pronounce them.

Once Mrs. Knight called on me to read in class, and I was doing just fine till I came to the word, "redress." By mistake, I accented the wrong syllable, so it came out sounding like "red ress." I tried to carry on as if nothing had happened, but Mrs. Knight made me stop.

"What was that word you said?"

I put my finger under that word and focused on it again. Then I remembered how to say it. "Redress!" That's the kind of help she gave me.

I also made covers for all my textbooks by cutting up old paper grocery bags. These covers became my note pads. In class, I jotted down words and ideas to memorize later, and when a book cover got full, I replaced it.

Math class at Dillard was really challenging, and the teacher let us use a calculator "to make it easier," or so she said. I'd worked with a calculator only a little bit before, but it wasn't easy for me to locate the buttons, and I had a hard time memorizing where they were. When I tapped in a number, I had to double-check every digit. Often, I had to clear and start over. So half the time, I just didn't use the calculator. Instead, I found my own ways to do math.

Addition was fairly straightforward. I did sums by counting on my fingers. To subtract, I drew dots on a page. Let's say I wanted to subtract 29 from 43. First I would draw 43 dots, counting them out loud as I went. Then I would erase 29 dots, again counting each one. After that, I would simply count the dots that were left. Multiplication took longer. For instance, to multiply 7 times 9, I would draw 7 sets of 9 dots. Then I would count all the dots out loud to get the final result. Let's don't even talk about how I managed to do long division. As you can imagine, my process was very slow, but it helped me gain a feel for how numbers worked.

Using a calculator didn't teach me about math. Instead, I made myself learn the actual steps of each calculation. The work was cumbersome and plodding, but it really helped. Some more advanced problems ran for eight or ten lines before the answer appeared. Deriving square roots, for instance. I eventually taught myself how to do that.

If you find this hard to believe, let me tell you about "dyscalculia." It's one more type of dyslexia that I've only recently learned about. People with this condition have difficulty processing basic addition and subtraction. Yet they're able to understand complex mathematical concepts. So, yes, I have to add one more condition to my list – dyscalculia.

Mrs. Knight and Mrs. Patton sometimes spent whole lunch periods helping me work through lessons, and their encouragement meant the world to me. I found ways to stay organized and focused, and I became obsessive about keeping lists, a habit I still retain. What I was doing, in fact, was learning how to learn.

After the first semester of my freshman year, my grade point average was 2.7, or C+. At the end of the second semester, my GPA came up an entire grade to 3.5, or B+. After that, I never made less than 3.9, and for the rest of my high school career, I took honors classes and made the honor roll every semester.

CHAPTER SIXTEEN

Both Attraction And Repulsion Inspire Us To Act

Training my body to be stronger, faster and tougher felt righteous, and it gave me a release to burn off stress. On basketball game nights, the sounds and smells of the gym energized me, and the chance to use my skills on the court gave me deep satisfaction. I loved to hustle, and our team did well. Soon, I grew a beard and wore my hair in long braids. I began to feel more comfortable with myself as an individual.

But Coach Rock kept warning me that, for all my talent, basketball would not be my game because I wasn't tall enough. Only through football, he said, would I earn my ticket out of the ghetto. More than once, I asked my parents if I could play, but they remained firm. They would not give permission.

It came to a head one day in the summer following my sophomore year. Dad, Mike and I were sitting outside in the front yard talking, and Mom was in the garage sewing. It was Saturday, an ordinary sunny day in Florida. A neighbor girl walked by, a high school senior named Keesha, and my dad called out to her in his friendly way. "Hey, how you doing?" he said.

Keesha stopped to talk. She was really excited because she'd just received a letter from Florida State University offering her a full basketball scholarship. Naturally, we all congratulated her.

Mike took a long time looking at her letter, as if he was devising some scheme. Mike had a gift as a con artist. After Keesha had gone, he said in his smooth-talking way, "Dad, don't you think Yo's as good an athlete as Keesha?"

"Sure he is," Dad said.

Mike said, "Well, don't you think Yo could get a football scholarship?"

Dad said, "Yo doesn't play football."

So I piped up. "I've always wanted to."

Mike kept working his point. "You want him to go to college, right? A scholarship would pay for everything."

Dad admitted that would be nice. He was in an easy mood that day.

So Mike turned to me and said, "What would you have to do to sign up?"

I had the answer ready. "We could go to the field right now. They've already started practice, and Coach Redman asked me to try out."

Dad shrugged and smiled. "Okay."

I couldn't believe it. Everything was happening so fast. We got in the car and drove to the field. I was sixteen years old, and as I've said before, I'd never played a single organized game of football in my life. I was scared to death.

When we got there, I introduce Dad and Mike to Coach Redman, then told him I had permission to try out. The coach said I would need a physical exam later, but he let me join the practice right then. An assistant coach took me to the locker room and fitted me with a helmet, pads, pants and an old set of cleats. I felt so happy, my whole body was shaking.

When I ran back out to the field, Coach said, "I need you to play right guard."

I said, "Coach, I want to play defensive line."

"It's right guard or no play," he said.

I just smiled. "Okay, that's what it'll be."

My friend Nigel was on the team, and he showed me

what to do. My nerves were jumping. Less than an hour earlier, I'd been at home in my yard daydreaming, and now – here I was trying out for football!

First, we did individual drills. Then we lined up and ran a toss play, the first live play of my life. My mind blanked out. The left guard was supposed to pull to the right, and I was supposed to block to the right. But in my confusion, I pulled left. He turned, I turned. We collided head on and both fell backward, hitting the dirt.

My first practice did not go well. Nevertheless, Coach gave me a pat on the back and let me bring my pads home. I tried not to dwell on the mistakes I'd made. When we got back to our house, Mom was standing in the open door.

"Where you been?" she said.

Dad didn't say anything, so Mike answered. "We went to Jovan's school."

"Why?" Mom came marching out toward us, and when she saw my pads, her face went dark.

"I went to football practice," I said.

She glared at my dad. Then she kissed her teeth at me, turned on her heel, and walked back into the house.

Mike and I snuck into my bedroom to hide out, but we could hear Mom yelling at Dad. When he retreated into the garage, she followed him.

After a few minutes, she shouted, "Yo, come here." I knew trouble was coming. Mom and I hadn't argued in quite a while because I'd learned to keep a low profile, but now she was enraged. When I walked out to face her, she poked me in the chest and shouted, "You devil boy! My opinion don't count? You totally disobey me?"

She didn't give me a chance to answer. She was screaming, cursing, using vulgar words. "You'll never be any good at football. Those kids been playing longer, and you can't catch up. You can't learn anything. Look at your grades."

I took a step back. "Mom, have you seen my grades? I'm on the honor roll. I'm trying to go to college."

"You just chasing girls," she said.

What did she mean? I didn't have a girlfriend. I never went out with girls, never even talked to girls on the phone. I turned to Dad for help, but he was staring at the TV, pretending not to hear us. So I stayed cool. I held everything in while she called me dirty names.

Finally she said, "If you break your neck, I won't think twice about you."

That's when I lost it. I started bawling.

"Aw, look at you. Always crying," she said.

I turned and walked away. My shoes were still in the car, and I was barefoot, but I walked an hour and half.

My thoughts turned very bleak that day. I wondered if my life was worth living. I felt angry at Dad because he'd left me hanging. Most of all, I felt sick with bitterness toward Mom.

That time she ran off to California and left Dad and me behind, she made it plain she didn't want a "dumb kid" for a son. Her words today reconfirmed it. When the one person who should be there for you is not there, it makes a hollow place inside. I thought about moving out, maybe sleeping on somebody's couch. I thought about killing myself. My hopes, what I wanted to do with my life, suddenly meant nothing.

But as I kept walking, my thoughts took a new direction. My mother's first abandonment had marked the beginning of our long slow rupture, and this day completed it. I realized I would never satisfy her, so why should I let her define me? My life did have worth, and I would prove it. That day changed everything for me because I resolved that I would excel at football, earn a full scholarship and graduate from college. Not only that. I would go on to the NFL.

CHAPTER SEVENTEEN

If We Practice Shifting Gears Long Enough, There's No Car We Can't Drive

After my big showdown with Mom, I came home from my walk, took a shower and went to bed without dinner. I didn't sleep well, but the next day, I had one hell of a practice. Football is a violent sport. A good play feels like two trains colliding, and when we play angry, we don't get tired. Our adrenaline comes from a different tank.

For a little while, I played solely out of anger. I focused on the prize –college, money, a life beyond the ghetto. I wanted to raise a family, start a business, help my relatives and people in need. More than anything, I wanted to prove my mother wrong. Football would open all those doors for me.

But in time, the sheer joy of playing the game took over. I rediscovered the pleasure of hard effort and the feeling of being part of something bigger. Then I began to play truly well. Learning the game came more easily than I'd expected, because I'd learned how to learn. Already I understood the concept of team strategy from basketball and soccer. I knew my role, and I trained for it. I played offensive right guard, where my prime duty was to protect the quarterback by blocking defensive tackles. I also blocked for ball carriers on running plays. I was fast and strong, and the guard position was a natural for me.

My happiest times were on the football field, and brother Mike was my biggest fan. Still, with an eye toward college, I kept my lists and did my homework. I really buckled down on class preparation and learned to map things out in my head. Finally I began to grasp more complex concepts in science and math. With football in one hand and academics in the other, everything became easier.

Nigel and I competed, on the field and also in class. At three hundred pounds, he was even bigger than me. Unlike me, he had always made good grades. We arranged to share as many classes as possible, and we studied together. Neither of us had girlfriends. We didn't hang out or go to parties. We went straight from class to football practice, then home to study. The one time I went to the skating rink with some teammates, there was a shoot-out. Never again, I decided. The places those guys went were places I didn't want to be.

In computer programming class, Nigel and I had a teacher who spoke with a strong Russian accent, and in his class, I sometimes made fun of the way he talked. Me making fun of someone's speech, can you believe it? Twice he sent me to the principal's office, but my jokes were meant to be friendly, and I think he knew that. After a while, he and I became friends. At lunch, he'd let Nigel and me use the computer lab to play StarCraft. I enjoyed learning to fix computers. In teams of four, we'd take an old computer apart, even the motherboard. Then we'd build a new computer from scratch. My job was soldering and plugging the wires accurately. I wrote my first basic program in his class, and when he said, "Good job!" it felt like a breakthrough.

Every year, we built a robot in his class for the state science fair, and twice we finished in the top three places. I liked working with the programming students because they were serious about learning. They thought football was super cool, but I thought they were the coolest kids I'd ever known. On some days, everyone in class would play against each other in one big game of StarCraft, and more than once, we missed the bus trying to finish. That class was fun.

Pretty soon, Nigel and I became so focused on academics that we were practically living like monks, and people began to crack jokes. "When you coming back down to earth?" they'd say. My teammates made fun of me for trying to speak proper English instead of using our local slang.

One girl said, "Why don't you date? All these girls like you, but you show them no attention."

At that time, I was still very shy of girls, so I tried to sidestep her. "There's somewhere I have to be."

Then she asked me to my face, "Are you gay?"

Why did she think that? I wondered. Because I studied and went to class? I just laughed and walked away. I told myself, keep doing what you're doing, and someday you'll get out of here. Every day I told myself: Get to college, get to the NFL, and be the man you want to be.

Meanwhile, at home, an air of negativity settled in our house. If Mom overheard Mike and me talking about football, she would kiss her teeth at me. She never looked at my report cards anymore, and I kept my distance from her. Eventually, our relationship smoothed over, but only on the surface. Underneath, my feelings for Mom would never be the same.

Dad and I bonded again fairly soon. He was quiet and non-confrontational, and I could tell he wanted us to be friends. That summer, he taught me how to drive a car. For me, learning to drive was almost as difficult as learning to read. On Saturdays, Dad and I would climb into the old brown Honda, the one our family had owned since I first moved to the States. It had a standard transmission, and I struggled to memorize the correct positions of the gearshift and the proper sequence of footwork.

Dad usually took me to an empty parking lot to practice, and his lessons were nerve-racking. When I stalled the engine, he'd lose patience and yell, "You're burning out the clutch!" This happened so often, I almost said, "To heck with it."

But I needed to drive, so I kept trying. Sometimes I'd sit in the parked car alone in our driveway, and I would simply go through the moves in my mind. I wouldn't turn the ignition on. I'd simply talk myself through the pedals and the gears again and again, burning it into my memory. This repetition helped.

To drive on an actual road, I needed a learner's permit, and that required passing a written test. In preparation, I read the study booklet backwards and forwards, but connecting the road sign symbols with their meanings was as tricky for me as my first efforts to read had been – matching a string of abstract letters with a picture of a cat.

Dad drove me to the testing center on a Saturday, when the lines were longest. We had to wait an hour and a half, and my anxiety increased with each passing minute. In the end, I failed the written test, not once but twice. Dad didn't say anything either time, but I knew he was angry.

On the third try, I passed, and we went for my first real drive. When Dad stopped at a traffic light and gave me the wheel, I felt so tense that my muscles stiffened up. When the light changed, I tried to ease the car into first gear, but it shot out through the intersection with a violent shudder and then stalled. My hands were shaking so hard, I couldn't re-start the ignition.

Dad said, "Come on, man, you gotta move!"

Mike was in the back seat laughing. Dad was fuming. I could not get the engine started. Finally Dad took over and drove us home. He was really disappointed in me that day.

Still, I kept practicing. Whenever I could, I drove the car around our neighborhood alone, and it was much easier without Dad looking over my shoulder. I practiced shifting and working the clutch until my moves became smooth every time. I mastered that standard transmission, and today there is not a stick shift I can't drive.

Once I got my license, Dad taught me how to parallel park on a steep hill. That was brutal, but I learned. When he saw my improvement, he let me drive the green Honda, which was newer and prettier than the old brown one. Man, I washed that car twice a week. I coated the vinyl surfaces with Armor-All, and I used Q-tips to clean the air vents. If I washed the car on Friday and it rained Saturday, I'd wash it again on Sunday. On weekends, I drove Mike and Barrington to the movies. I ran errands for Mom and Dad. I fell in love with driving.

Dad didn't approve of everything I did, though. For instance, he often criticized my long braids. A family friend did my braids in the newest designs and patterns, and I thought my braids looked awesome, but Dad felt long hair belonged only on women. Maybe if I'd worn Jamaican dreadlocks, he might have been more accepting.

CHAPTER EIGHTEEN

If You Can't Climb The Tree, Then Use A Stick To Reach The Fruit

All along, Mike and I had been spending our summers in Jamaica, staying with Auntie Cynthia, Audia and Neshia. But that summer, we made only a brief visit. Toll Gate no longer gave me the same thrill as before. It seemed different, although in reality, I was the one who'd changed.

All my cousins were growing up. Some went to summer school, and some had jobs in May Pen. Three of them had died. Even Gareth left Toll Gate in summers to stay with his cousins in the mountains where the days were cooler. Audia and Neshia both had jobs and boyfriends. There was no one around to play soccer or anything else.

What's more, the outdoors was no longer a place of carefree liberty. In the cane fields and woods, I started notic-ing thorns, rusted wire and broken glass. No way would I run barefoot. I kept my shoes on. Whereas we used to catch fish and shrimp from the canals to fry in a pan, now I wouldn't think of eating anything from those stagnant canals. In the States, I'd learned about poison ivy and spiders. The fact was, I'd begun to develop more phobias.

Learning to swim had helped me face my fear of water, but my fear of flying had been getting steadily worse. And I'd also began to fear heights. The guinep trees were full of ripe fruit, but the idea of climbing panicked me. All I could think about was falling and breaking my bones. When I was younger, I fell a few times and banged myself up hitting branches, but I just shook off the pain and climbed the tree again. My new phobia put an end to the joy of climbing But that summer I used a forked stick to reach the fruit – just one of many work-arounds I've had to learn.

Researchers have found a high correlation between dyslexia and certain phobias. Some experts think both conditions may stem from flawed processing of visual cues. Just as written text appears to float off the page, so objects in space become jumbled and confused, and the resulting disorientation can lead to fear of heights, flying, swimming and other motion-related phobias. Yes, I can testify to that.

Jamaican traffic scared me, too, and for good reason. The taxi-van conductors careened through town at ninety miles an hour, sometimes forcing other cars off the road. Those vans packed in so many people, it was incredible. A single van might carry twenty passengers, sitting in each other laps or even hanging outside the vehicle. There were no sidewalks, no speed limits, and pedestrians stood way too close to the road. It made me tense just to watch.

Without a doubt, the lighthearted summers of my childhood were gone. Many times that last summer in Toll Gate, Mike and I would walk from house to house and find no one there. So we'd just sit around on Auntie Cynthia's porch. With no cousins, no fishing or climbing, no gun war in the cane fields, we passed our days in boredom. After that summer, Mike and I made only short visits to Toll Gate with our parents. As I write this, I'm planning my first return in thirteen years.

Still, we didn't have to fly across the Caribbean to experience old Jamaica. All we had to do was ride twenty minutes to Sistrunk to see our grandpa. Sistrunk was another Ft. Lauderdale ghetto, worse than ours. Prostitutes walked the streets, and cops often found dead bodies along the train tracks. I saw a dead body once, and many times I heard the crack of gunfire. Hundreds of bullet cases littered the sidewalks from drive-by shootings, and Grandpa kept a submachine gun by his front door. Crack cocaine was turning Sistrunk into a battleground.

But everyone loved my grandpa, even the thugs. Nobody bothered him. When I was sixteen, he was in his sixties, a big-bellied man with a missing front tooth and long braids pulled tight over his bald spot. People called him Teeco, or Teeks for short. He was my dad's father, and he lived as if he were still in Toll Gate. He drank rum all day, and he spoke with a strong island accent. On Sundays, he'd cook pounds of curried goat and rice for everybody in the 'hood.

Part of his window was missing, and vermin reigned in his house. Rats, mice and cockroaches roamed freely. While he was in the midst of cooking, he'd spray Raid insecticide all around his stove to drive them away. His kitchen would not have passed any inspection, but that didn't stop us from enjoying his delicious food. Dad took Mike and me to visit him every weekend, and Grandpa kept a stock of grape and strawberry soda just for us.

I don't believe he was involved in the drug trade, but people took care of him. He kept a drawer full of cash, which he often shared with Mike and me. He was the one who had named me Yovan, although he pronounced it "Ovan." He could have lived in a nicer place, and Dad often urged him to move, but Grandpa felt Sistrunk was home. He's still alive as I write this, and I know that if I offered him a fine mansion, he wouldn't take it. That's one thing I love about Teeks.

CHAPTER NINETEEN

Don't Buy Your Pizzas Too Soon

What a change my last two years of high school made. I took advanced placement classes in preparation for college, and I earned straight A's. Along with good grades, I also dominated on the football field. Both years, I earned first-team All-State honors, and I have to believe my success on the field fueled my turnaround in academics.

Coach Redman arranged to take his best players to football camps to meet other high school teams and show what we could do. My first camp was at Michigan State. On Friday afternoon, about a dozen of us loaded into a couple of vans, and we drove late into the night to get there. The camp was held on Saturday, and the first thing I noticed was the grass. East Lansing had the greenest grass I'd ever seen. The campus was gorgeous, and I noticed that we were one of the few mostly black teams there.

When camp started, we ran drills and lifted weights. Then we played 7-on-7 flag football, a no-contact form of the game. We did our best to demonstrate our talents to the coaches, and I was voted "hardest worker." Afterward, we toured the campus facilities and met the Michigan State football team and coaches. On Sunday, we drove home, talking football the whole way. Altogether, I attended two camps at Michigan State, two at Auburn, and one at Miami.

Dillard High School played in Division 6a, Florida's highest ranked division, and in my senior year, I played in the All-Star game of Dade County versus Broward County. It was a thrilling game, and although we lost, I felt that we performed well. I was named Most Valuable Player on Offense, and I was one of only two players in Florida to make All-State Guard.

Early in my senior year, the college letters started arriving, and soon, I was getting hundreds of letters. They came from all over the country, from every college you can name. Mike was ecstatic, and my parents wanted to celebrate, but most of the letters were computer-generated forms expressing generic interest in my football talents. Yet some letters were hand-written, and those were the real ones. My first hand-written note came from Lloyd Carr, head coach at the University of Michigan. "I'll be watching you," he wrote.

Then more hand-written notes appeared. They came from Michigan State, Ohio State, Auburn, Georgia, Miami. But even personal letters didn't mean anything until an actual scout showed up to meet you.

Sure enough, during our fall practice, the scouts started arriving. Coach Redman had a reputation as one of the best high school coaches in Florida, and hundreds of scouts came to watch his team every year. We might have fifty scouts at any single game. Their presence made me play better, because I knew their judgment spelled my opportunity.

One Thursday, Coach Redman called me to his office after school and introduced me to a scout from the University of Miami. The scout was selecting players from all over the state to see Miami play Florida State at the Orange Bowl. I was trembling with excitement. This was my first real meeting with a scout.

We sat down in Coach's office, and as soon as the scout started talking football, I relaxed. When he asked about my grades and SAT scores, I told him the truth. My scores on timed tests were always low, but my grade point average was 4.5, and that impressed him. Of course I didn't mention dyslexia. He asked about my financial situation, my family, if I was willing to move to another city, if I had a girlfriend. He wanted to know what other schools I planned to visit.

After our meeting, I felt on top of the world. Of course I accepted his invitation to see the game at the Orange Bowl. The day before the game, the selected players traveled to Miami to tour the stadium and meet the team. Then we sat in a special section to watch the game. It was spectacular.

Many other meetings with scouts followed that first one. At that time, several of my magnet school friends were stressing over college applications, but I never had to apply to college. I ended up with so many scholarship offers, I almost couldn't choose.

Every scholarship offer came with an invitation to visit the campus, but the NCAA allowed each student athlete to make only five official college visits. Otherwise, students might miss too much class time. My first campus visit required an airline flight over the Appalachian Mountains to Marshall University in Huntsville, West Virginia. That trip further underscored my phobia of flying.

The first leg was easy. I rode on a huge commercial airliner, and the weather was clear. But in Atlanta, I changed to a connector aircraft with only six passenger seats. It was like going from a Rolls Royce to a Pinto. Apparently, our destination airport in West Virginia couldn't accommodate a larger plane.

From that point on, the scenario seemed to come straight out of a horror movie. We took off in a storm, and the winds tossed the airplane like a paper kite. Lightning flashed around us, the sky grew dark, and the unpredictable turbulence made my head reel. I gripped the seatback in front of me, sweating and praying, close to panic.

While we were still in the storm, the stewardess told me about a plane carrying thirty-seven Marshall football players that had crashed in the mountains in 1970. "It was famous," she said. But I was thinking, "Dear Lord, why are you telling me this?" When I glimpsed the snow covered mountains below, I shut my eyes.

To my amazement, we landed safely, and the long drive to the campus was pleasant and scenic. The best thing about that visit was seeing my name on the Jumbotron. "Marshall University Welcomes Jovan Haye!" That was the coolest thing I'd ever seen. A couple of the football players took me to a campus party that night, and we saw two sorority girls fighting. I'd never seen girls fight that way, and I wondered, "Is this what people do in college?"

That very weekend, Marshall made me an offer. The coach said, "Jovan, you'll be the cornerstone of our defense for years to come."

His words flattered me, but I didn't want to rush. Instead, I promised to think it over. After I left, the Marshall staff called me for two weeks straight to see if I'd made a decision.

Over the next few weeks, I visited other campuses to check out the facilities and meet the staff. It was a unique experience to see the different places where I might live. All told, I received firm offers from Michigan State, Miami, Western Michigan, Marshall, Auburn, Ohio State and Vanderbilt University.

Nigel got a lot of offers, too, and he decided on Georgia Tech because of its excellent academic program. But one Friday I came to class and found him looking depressed.

"What's up?" I asked.

He said, "Man, Georgia Tech cancelled."

He didn't have to say anything more. I knew what he was feeling. "Something better will come along," I told him.

That very day, a scout invited us to visit Vanderbilt University for the weekend. I was scheduled to visit Ohio State, but I cancelled my trip in order to go with Nigel.

Nigel liked Vanderbilt at first sight. We stayed over till Sunday, and when he decided to sign a letter of intent to play with the Vanderbilt Commodores, I did, too. It was a snap decision, guided only by instinct. I knew zero about Vanderbilt football. I didn't know their uniform colors. I didn't even know what conference they played in. All I knew was that a guy from Dillard was already playing there.

When I made my announcement at the press conference, cameras were flashing, and reporters were taking notes. I said, "I'm going to the University of Vanderbilt." I didn't even know the school's proper name. Nigel had to tell me later.

Not long after that, the Dillard player called me and said, "Coming to Vanderbilt was the biggest mistake of my life." He said other universities gave strong support to football and had a winning tradition, but not Vanderbilt. He made me second-guess my choice.

But I'd always been a dreamer. The Vanderbilt scout had assured me that they were rebuilding their program from the ground up, and I wanted to be part of that. Starting from the bottom and rising to the top, that held a special appeal for me. I pictured our team on the cover of *Sports Illustrated.*

With that decision made, my mind was at ease. My magnet friends were fretting about their grades and waiting for decisions on academic scholarships. Me, I had a full athletic scholarship to Vanderbilt University worth $50,000 a year. Vanderbilt's academic program was first-rate, I'd heard. I didn't yet know how demanding it would be.

That spring, I went to the Dillard prom dressed in a white dinner jacket and black evening pants – like James Bond. My long braids hung neatly down my back. I stood 6'2", with 225 pounds of well-trained muscle. My date, a girl named Tina, was just 4'11", so you can imagine what a couple we made. I had a crush on Tina, but since I was neither a dancer nor a party guy, the prom turned out to be our one and only date.

As senior year was ending, Mom finally acknowledged my football achievement by attending one game, my final game in high school. We were competing for the State Championship, and everyone knew we would win because ours was the most dominant team in Florida. In fact, we were so confident that, on game day, Coach Redman ordered seventy pizzas for our victory feast.

In the Gainesville stadium, we faced our toughest challengers, the Palm Bay Pirates from Melbourne, Florida. My Vanderbilt scholarship was a done deal, and I was feeling good. The Pirates played well, and near the end, the score was close, but all the odds remained in our favor. As the final seconds counted down, we lined up for our winning touchdown. It was an easy play we couldn't miss – yet we did. When the pass was incomplete, no one could believe it. A full twelve seconds elapsed before the Pirates realized they'd won.

By then, our whole team was crying, and when we were called up to receive our second-place medals, I was still crying. Mom called to me from the sidelines. "What does it matter, Yo? You've already got your scholarship."

I wanted no part of her consolation. I hated losing. Overconfidence had defeated us, and I felt enormous regret that we could not turn back the clock and run that play again. I cried on the bus all the way back to the hotel where we were staying.

That night, seventy pizzas went into the hotel pool. My teammates vented their disappointment by running riot, and I'm sorry to say I did, too. We pulled fire alarms, set off smoke detectors, broke beds and doors. We weren't drinking. We were simply maddened by remorse and humiliation. Later, our high school principal sent us a hefty bill for the damages, and all the money we'd set aside to buy our football rings went instead to pay the hotel.

For me, as for many young people, high school graduation day was both proud and sad. A major accomplishment lay behind me, and a huge unknown lurked ahead. All my Florida relatives came to the ceremony. Auntie Dahlia and Uncle Woody came down from Jersey. That night, a lot of kids went to Orlando for a big graduation party, but my parents didn't approve. That didn't matter to me. High school was over. I was so ready to move on.

CHAPTER TWENTY

Acceptance Is Its Own Kind Of Victory

Before I could complete my enrollment at Vanderbilt, I had to become a US citizen. My parents had become naturalized citizens years earlier, and my brother was born in the US. Only I still lacked citizenship. The naturalization process entailed a written test about American facts, history and law, an interview with the US Immigration Service, and a formal oath of loyalty. So in June, 2001, Dad took me to Miami to undergo this exhausting, yet exhilarating, rite of passage.

Dad got me a study book with sample questions, and though I found it difficult to read, the subject interested me. I'd lived in the States most of my life, and I'd recently studied American history in high school, so I wasn't worried about the test. The interview, though, was another story.

The parking situation was horrendous around the Miami Immigration office, and we had to walk a long way from our car. Dad waited in the hall while I anxiously went through my one-on-one interrogation. The interviewing officer asked questions like how did I get to the US, had I ever done drugs, and were any of my relatives involved in illegal drug traffic. Despite my jumpy nerves, the interview went well because I gave honest answers.

Afterward came the test. To my great relief, I passed, and three hours later, I joined a group of about two hundred people to swear the oath of citizenship. This included the Pledge of Allegiance, plus a solemn vow to abide by all US laws and to work hard to become a prosperous citizen. As I spoke the final words of the oath, a shiver ran through my body.

US citizenship conveys enormous privilege and security. Without it, an immigrant walks on pins and needles, constantly worried about paying his annual fees, overstaying his visit, or letting his green card expire. Even a legal alien can be deported for any infraction of the law. I knew Jamaicans who'd been sent back to the island for minor crimes, forever banned from the possibility of US citizenship. Though I've continued to maintain dual citizenship in Jamaica and the US, achieving my American citizenship made me feel safe.

Soon after that, I packed for college. My parents seemed enthusiastic about my enrollment at Vanderbilt, and just before we went, they bought me a desktop computer and printer, a small TV and some new bedding. Then we rented a van and loaded up for the drive to Nashville.

I arrived on campus in summer, weeks ahead of the main student body. All the freshmen athletes came early for training camp, both girls and guys. Vanderbilt had teams for baseball, basketball, lacrosse, soccer, tennis and some other sports. During training camp, the athletes stayed in a dorm called the Towers, and on the first day, I met a cute girl in the elevator, although we didn't actually talk till a couple weeks later. I shared a room with two other freshmen, but mostly we camped out in a suite shared by some older players.

On my earlier visit, I hadn't seen the whole campus. Vanderbilt covered over three hundred acres, with countless quadrangles, large old trees, and red brick buildings dating from the late 1800's. The university contained ten different colleges, and the student body numbered more than six thousand. But in summer, except for us athletes, the place was empty.

Summer training camp was supposed to help freshmen athletes get accustomed to college life, and yet college life hadn't started. I had no car, no way to get around unless someone gave me a ride. All I had was football.

On our first meeting day, the football staff came into our dorm banging pots and pans and blowing an air horn at 5:30 am. Still groggy with sleep, we rushed over to the football facility to sign in for breakfast. After a quick shower, we changed into workout shorts and shirts, got our wrists and ankles taped, and went to the team meeting. The coaches explained our agenda for the day, and then we did hard practice for two and a half hours.

After morning practice, we had a short mid-day break, during which we could: 1) sit in an ice tub; 2) eat lunch in the cafeteria; or 3) grab a snack and go back to the dorm to sleep. For the first few days, I chose option number three.

I had a system to wake up after lunch, because I absolutely did not want to be late. First, I set an alarm on my computer, then on my cell phone, and then on my clock. Plus I asked a teammate to call me, just to be sure. In the afternoon, we had another two and a half hours of grueling practice. Then we were done for the day.

For the first two weeks, I took my evening meals in my room and went straight to sleep. But after getting used to the routine, I felt less exhausted. The girl I'd met in the elevator turned out to be friendly, and we often talked on the phone at night. She soon became my first college girlfriend.

In time, I started eating in the cafeteria and hanging out with the other players. When we weren't practicing, we sat around watching TV, surfing the web, or playing video games. We hung out in the dorm lobby killing time, or sometimes we walked across the street to eat at Chili's. Not surprisingly, this routine soon got boring.

Vanderbilt has long been known for outstanding academics, but it may surprise you to learn that Vandy also ranks as a top party school. As I write this, Vanderbilt ranks seventh in the nation for partying. That summer, I went to my first Vanderbilt party, the first of many more to come. Almost everyone at the party was black. Most were athletes, and many were juniors and seniors. The college girls looked so mature and sophisticated, they intimidated me. I stood in a corner and kept quiet.

That night was the first time I tasted alcohol. It was mixed in some kind of fruit punch, so the flavor was sweet. Because I had no tolerance, the alcohol went straight to my head. I didn't like the feeling of being intoxicated and losing control, so I didn't drink much. Still, the drink left me with a splitting headache. You would think it might have been a lesson to me. Too bad it wasn't.

At the party that night, I met a football player named A-Mac. He was a junior, and we started talking about life. I told him I wanted to study mechanical engineering. That's what Nigel was studying, and it sounded like a good plan to me.

He said, "You sure, man? Vandy's hard, especially engineering."

"Yeah, I'm not gonna let anyone deter me," I told him.

He said, "You like to study? You like to get up early? Engineering's gonna consume a lot of time, and you've got football, too. You won't be going to parties. You'll be a zombie, man."

"I'm pretty sure I'll be okay," I told him.

"Listen," he said, "I was in mechanical engineering my freshman year, and I had to switch because the workload was too much. You think about it."

That conversation made me reconsider my plan, and later, I was glad he enlightened me. In the end, my advisor steered me to the Human and Organizational Development major, which proved to be the right choice for me.

As the monotonous days of summer dragged on, I worked hard at football, but I didn't know the other players well. One day after practice, I stood at an upper window in the Towers looking out at the empty campus with its vacant quads and deserted buildings. All at once, I didn't want to be there. I missed my brother, my friends, my life. I missed people. Before that summer, I thought homesickness was a joke, but suddenly I was wiping away tears. When the feeling passed, I told myself never to look out that window again.

Soon after that, though, my life got better. A small tight-knit group formed within the larger football squad, nine freshman players, all black, and I found myself among them. We came from different backgrounds and had different goals. Maybe it was the shared tedium that drew us together. We called ourselves "2-Trill" because we were "too true and real for college." Sure, we were full of ourselves.

The guy who named our group was Cheron, also called C.T. or Cat Man. He was about 5'8", very muscular, very outgoing. He had a good heart, and he loved to joke around. Also, he was bright and curious. He liked to observe how society was put together, and once after college, he lived for a while as a homeless man in order to write a book. Recently, he talked about walking all the way to Arizona to raise money for charity. At Vandy, he and I became close friends, and he was my roommate for sophomore year.

The brains of our group was Kelechi, aka Q. Kelechi's parents were Nigerian. He grew up in Texas, wore dreads and had an opinion about everything. He enjoyed deep conversations on wide-ranging topics. He and I were roommates in our junior year, and as I write this, he's attending law school.

Moses, or Mo, was a Nashvillian, quiet and reserved. His parents were also Nigerian, and he also wore long dreadlocks. His mother was a police officer, and she raised him to be a serious, diligent student. In addition, he was an outstanding athlete, having won multiple high school championships. Mo had a truck, which 2-Trill often used to get around town.

Dominique, or Nicko, came from Nashville, too. He was moody and tended to go his own way. Sometimes he disappeared for long stretches, and he left Vandy midway through his junior year.

Keith came from Atlanta. He was a loud guy, flashy but not arrogant. He had pockets full of money, a nice car and stylish clothes, and he was generous. Once he invited us to his family's mansion in Atlanta, and he paid for everything. But later, his dad lost all the money, and Keith had to drop out of Vandy in his sophomore year. I believe he finished up at a community college in Atlanta.

Jerrin, or Chin, had money as well. He came from Texas, and he'd played against Kelechi in high school. The tallest of our group, Chin spoke with a thick Texas drawl, and he said whatever was on his mind, even if it sounded rude. After two years at Vandy, he decided he didn't like the position he was playing, so he transferred to Middle Tennessee State University. Later, he became a model in fitness magazines.

Ronnie, the Squirrel Man, hated his nickname because we said he looked like a squirrel. He came from Athens, Georgia, and his dad, uncle and brother were all great athletes. He was an infamous jokester, and he had no shame. One summer, my brother Mike came to visit, and Ronnie took him around the dorm, knocking on all the girls' doors and singing songs to whoever answered.

Brandon's nickname was B-Sweet. He came from Baton Rouge, and he spoke in a soft Cajun accent. We loved to hear him talk. Tall, skinny and quiet, he was a good athlete, and he was the only one in our group who chose the College of Arts and Sciences. The rest of us ended up in Peabody College, majoring in Human and Organizational Development.

My 2-Trill name was Jungle, the same as in high school. Being part of 2-Trill gave me enormous pleasure. I felt at home with those guys. I could be myself. This was the first time since playing with my cousins in Jamaica that I felt really accepted.

CHAPTER TWENTY-ONE

For An Athlete, The Game Comes First

After summer training camp, I made a quick visit to Florida, and when I came back to Nashville, to my amazement, the entire campus had changed. Instead of wide empty lawns and silent halls, Vanderbilt was full of motion, noise and people. The students had arrived in full force, a sea of fresh rosy white faces in prep-school clothing, and I was like a deer in headlights.

My parents helped me move into my co-ed freshman dorm in the Branscomb Quad. That same day, I signed up for classes, met my academic advisor, and went to the football facility to check in. Our family ate lunch with Nigel and his parents, and later, we found our way to the Green Hills Mall, where I bought my very first cell phone. It was cheap model with a terrible green screen, but I was thrilled because it meant independence. We window-shopped for a while, and then my parents dropped me off at my dorm and headed back to Florida. It was a long exciting day.

That first semester, I didn't have a roommate, and it was a rare treat to enjoy such privacy. I set up my room with tasteful accessories to match my new bedding. At first, I tried pushing the two single beds together, but they slipped apart during the night, and I fell between them. Still, that didn't dampen the joy of having a room to myself.

Right away, I discovered that Vanderbilt classes were far more demanding than classes at Dillard High School. Papers had to be based on solid research, following specific standards for references and footnotes. That was new to me, and I found it tedious. When I printed my essays, I used wide margins and a larger font so my writing covered more pages. For class presentations, I'd put together a PowerPoint show and read the slides word for word. The confidence I'd gained at Dillard was slipping.

On top of that, my girlfriend turned out to be a summer fling. We broke up early in the semester. "You need to experience real college life," she said. "You don't need to be tied down." Nevertheless, she warned me about the other girls on campus. "Be careful," she said, "they'll date you just because they think you'll go pro and make a lot of money."

Not many black girls attended Vanderbilt, and a lot of them had boyfriends at other Nashville colleges like Fisk, Meharry, and Tennessee State University. The white girls at Vanderbilt seemed so preppy and strange that I didn't know how to talk to them. At some level, I'd been hoping to meet my future wife at college, but things did not look promising.

At any rate, I had 2-Trill. We shared classes, rooms, football. We were always together, rising early for team meetings, sweating through workouts, rushing to classes, then rushing back for more practice. We made friends with some female basketball players, too, and they often hung out with us. They used to bake cakes for everyone's birthday. We cooked for each other, played video games and went to parties. In freshman year, I learned to stay up late at night because I didn't want to miss anything. As a result, I was always fighting exhaustion.

Sometimes at team meetings, when Coach handed out plays and talked about our game plan, I'd stand up through the whole discussion just to stay awake. We'd watched film of our previous practices and of others team we had to play. Everything in the meetings had a purpose, and I respected that purpose. I tried to pay attention. I loved the game. Yet football, too, was a lot more demanding in college than in high school.

Freshman players had low status in the squad, and most of us didn't expect to play our first year. Then came a breakthrough. For the first time, Coach asked me to run plays with the second team as an outside linebacker, a position I'd never played before. Linebackers play behind the defensive line, covering the receiver, rushing the passer, and defending against running plays. I rehearsed the linebacker's upright stance – slightly bent at the waist, feet apart, knees bent, hands forward, elbows tight to my ribs, with my weight centered over the balls of my feet so I'd be ready to lunge.

During practice, I performed so well that Coach told me to run plays with the first team. Afterward, he called me in for a talk. "We're not going to red-shirt you this year," he said. "We want you to start as an outside linebacker."

For those who don't know the term "redshirt," it means a one-year delay in college athletic participation. Most freshmen athletes are redshirted their first year, meaning they take classes but do not play. The Southeastern Conference is seriously competitive, so an extra year gives freshmen more time to prepare. Plus, it spreads their scholarship out for five years instead of four. Starting play as a freshman, especially in the Southeastern Conference, is rare. But the coach wanted me to start!

I was thrilled. I told everyone. Surely, this would be my ticket to the NFL. At the next practice, I was bouncing around, ready to show my talent. In one of our first plays, a receiver cut across me, and I grabbed for him with my left arm. In the same instant, a defensive tackle came running up behind me like a train locomotive. He knocked the receiver so flat, the guy's contact lenses flew out of his eyes. In the process, he also dislocated my left shoulder.

The pain was excruciating, especially when the team doctor had to twist and turn my arm several times to pop the joint back into place. Everyone could see it was a bad dislocation, and later, the MRI showed my muscle and cartilage had been torn from the bone. The doctor said

I would need surgery, rehab therapy and a long recovery period. My hope sank.

Still, I tried to play. I'd studied hard for the linebacker position, and I knew the chance might not come again. The doctor put me in a special brace so I could continue practice. But the brace limited my motion too much, and the pain made my eyes water. After my second practice, Coach and I agreed it was no go. He redshirted me, and two days later, I underwent shoulder surgery.

Now I see it as a blessing in disguise because my left shoulder grew stronger and more solid than ever. At the time, though, I felt totally unanchored. I couldn't even practice, so a whole year would be wasted. After such high hopes, I'd lost everything in a moment. It was like being cut from the team.

For five weeks after surgery, the pain in my joint persisted. The doctor prescribed a pain killer called oxycontin, an opiate drug, so for a while, I lived in la-la land. My shoulder had to be braced tight to my ribs to be fully immobilized, and I couldn't lift my arm to get a proper shower. Never had I felt more dirty than during that time. I missed many classes, and when I did go, I sensed people covering their noses. After the brace came off, I did rehab therapy three hours a day for months on end, but at least I could take a shower.

Though football was out for me, I still attended home games and sat on the bench to show support. That year, Vanderbilt kept losing game after game, which only added to my depression. I am not a fan of losing. At times, it seemed as if some of my teammates simply lacked the commitment to win. Most of them had football scholarships, yet they were skipping practices or coming late, focusing on tests and papers instead of learning the plays. They were putting football second to academics.

Of course academics are important, but for people who want to excel as athletes, the game has to come first. Athletic excellence requires hard study, rigorous training and total devotion. It's every bit as demanding as an academic program, and I felt that if a person accepted a full athletic scholarship, he also accepted an obligation to do his best. At Vanderbilt, however, too many of my teammates were not fulfilling that obligation.

This doubt was confirmed by an enlightening conversation I had when we played the University of Florida. This was the only away game I attended all year. I was still wearing my brace at that time, sitting on the bench in my sweats, trying not to show my irritation because we were losing so badly.

At half time, a police officer who was working security came over to talk to me. He was a Florida fan, and of course we talked about football. Our team had flown down to Gainesville on a charter, and at one point, he said, "I heard they served baloney on your charter flight."

I laughed. "Yeah, they did."

"They'd never do that here," he said. "We give our guys steak."

I tried to keep laughing, not to show how I really felt. Our team never got steak.

He said, "You Vanderbilt guys may be better than us Monday through Friday, but what counts here is Saturday."

I knew what his words meant. The University of Florida team put football first. If only Vanderbilt had more players who loved Saturday, maybe we wouldn't have lost that game by a score of 77 to 14.

CHAPTER TWENTY-TWO

Never Assume You've Made It Just Because You've Achieved One Goal

By the time my shoulder brace came off, I'd fallen far behind in class work. Unlike high school, there were no progress reports in college, no daily homework assignments, and few tests except the final exam. The only assignment might be to write three papers by the end of the semester. It was easy to tell myself I had plenty of time to catch up.

Besides, it was more fun to party with 2-Trill. At home, I'd been sheltered from parties and social life. But here I was, nineteen years old and on my own, with no parents telling me what to do – and more crucially, no football to keep me centered. Like many freshmen, I began to test my new freedom.

For three weeks, I dipped snuff. Then I started smoking "Black & Mild" cigarillos. Also, I began drinking more. Since the taste of alcohol repelled me, I learned to mix it with fruit punch or orange juice. Soon I was partying with 2-Trill several nights a week. Frankly, I let college get the best of me that year.

Naturally, my academics suffered. It was easy to skip class because professors rarely called roll. And many of my classes were so large that I could slide down behind the back row of auditorium seats and snooze. One day, I was sound asleep when a kid kicked my foot and said, "Wake up, man. You're snoring too loud."

If I stayed awake during class, chances were I'd be talking to my friends. Between classes, we'd have beer and smoke breaks. When we actually did try to write papers, we drank to make the work more bearable.

Before long, 2-Trill got a bad reputation on campus. We'd come to class late and sit on the back row of the auditorium, talking and showing attitude. Sometimes, other students would tell us to pipe down, and sometimes the professor would ask us to excuse ourselves from class. No one wanted us involved in their group projects. In part, I think our behavior was a defense mechanism.

For one thing, we sensed that no one respected us. Few Vanderbilt professors or students knew or cared about the demanding obligations of football. They seemed to view us as typical jocks, freeloading our way through college while playing a trivial game. For another thing, we looked different from other Vandy kids. For the most part, they were affluent white preppies, while we were just the opposite. Money was tight for most of us, so we didn't have the latest clothes, shoes and haircuts. Many athletes wore team-issued sweats and windbreakers to class.

Picture me, for example. Mom had sewn me four pairs of plaid cotton pajama bottoms for college. They were baggy and comfortable, with elastic waistbands, and for convenience, I wore them to class, usually with sleeveless muscle shirts called "wife beaters." Pajama-style clothing was trendy at that time, and they made getting dressed in the morning a lot easier. Also, if I didn't take care of my hair, my braids would frizz and look wild. Cheron and I competed over whose hair was longest. We met some girls at Tennessee State University who knew how to braid hair, but when they graduated and left Nashville, we found no one else who would do it for free.

People told me later that some white students were afraid of me. Maybe I looked menacing in my baggy pajamas, muscle shirts and unraveling braids. Also, I kept to myself, so people must have thought I was rude and mean. All of that made me less interested in going to class, and more eager to hang with 2-Trill.

On a typical day, we'd talk by cell and decide where to meet up for a night of partying. Around 8:00 pm, we'd gather in someone's dorm suite to have a few drinks before going out. Since we rarely had much money, our preferred drink was cheap Taaka vodka mixed with orange juice.

After three drinks or so, we'd leave around 11:00 pm and walk to a fraternity party. Every night of the week, somewhere on the Vanderbilt campus, there was a fraternity party. At first, we went to the all-black parties, but later we branched out. The white fraternities had more money, and their parties were epic. They brought in big name bands. One house brought in 2 Live Crew, a hip hop band from Florida.

It was during these parties that I first began to interact with the white student body. When I actually started talking to white kids, I felt more comfortable with them. They were not so different from me. One night, a blond girl said to me, "I didn't know you were this cool."

Troy Corby, my friend from Cliffside, had introduced me to rock music, so I felt at home with its rhythms. Drinking loosened me up, and the next thing you know, I started dancing. Picture me at 275 pounds, jumping and whirling around the middle of the dance floor. The other 2-Trill guys didn't dance much. Mostly they just drank and hung out with the other athletes, and my dancing made them laugh. Cheron told me, "You look like a dancing bear."

Every fraternity had its own signature drink, often as sweet as candy. As the night wore on, we'd have more drinks, and we'd make out with random girls. Everything would go blurry, and sometime around dawn, we'd stagger back across campus to our dorm rooms, crash into our beds, and sleep through our first classes of the day.

After a few weeks of this, I stopped getting hangovers because my body developed a tolerance for alcohol. At one party, I drank eight cups of punch and felt only a light buzz. In time, I began to mix vodka in my Gatorade bottle and take it with me to class. Sometimes I worried that I was becoming an alcoholic.

By football season's end, Vanderbilt had lost every game but two, and rumors were circulating that the coaching staff might be fired. This was bad news for me. I had no track record in college to prove my worth, and the new staff wouldn't know my capabilities. I worried they might not let me play.

At about the same time, our first semester ended, and our grades were dismal. Eight out of nine members of 2-Trill were placed on academic suspension. Only Kelechi made the grades needed to maintain his football scholarship. My grade point average was 1.8, and I was in danger of being dropped from the team and kicked out of college. That got my attention.

Too many outstanding athletes from neighborhoods like mine arrive at college unprepared. When they earn a full scholarship, they assume they've made it. Then they lose their way, flunk out and have to go right back to the same environment they were hoping to escape. I didn't want that future.

Three factors helped me stay on course. One was my own fear of losing my dream. To reach the NFL, I resolved to change my attitude and show more maturity. I had to work harder.

Two was the change in coaching staff. The rumors proved to be well founded, and in the early months of 2002,

Bobby Johnson came in as head coach, with new staff and bold new plans. He was upset to learn so many of his top players were on academic suspension, so he ordered us to check in for study hall every morning and to meet with tutors. He also demanded more oversight from our advisors.

The third factor was Mrs. Elizabeth Wright. Mrs. Wright was an academic advisor in the sports program. She wasn't my own advisor, but everyone talked about how understanding she was, and her kids did well in school. Mrs. Wright was about fifty, with long brown hair and an open friendly nature. She kept a drawer full of candy, and she welcomed any student who wanted to talk. When I asked her for help, she said yes.

I went often to see her. I told her private stuff, knowing my secrets would be safe. For me, she became like family. She went to bat for me, helped me pick the right classes, even got me into closed classes. She deserves most of the credit for helping me bring up my grades. Partying and social life continued to distract me, and I was far from a perfect student. Nevertheless, by year's end, my GPA was back to a solid C, back in the safe zone.

CHAPTER TWENTY-THREE

Welcome To The Jungle!

The summer after my freshman year, the team doctor cleared me to return to play, so along with other 2-Trill members, I stayed on campus for football practice. The coming season would mark our first real year of college football, our "redshirt freshman year." It was an exciting time but I couldn't help being anxious. I still didn't know what Coach Johnson intended for me.

In one of our first off-season workouts, David Turner, the new defensive line coach, walked over to me and said, "You're the one everybody's excited about."

His words caught me by surprise. I shrugged and said, "I don't pay attention to that."

"Come with me." He motioned me toward the defensive line, or D-line.

"I thought I'd play linebacker," I said.

He put his hands on his hips. "We've got a lot of good linebackers. Do you want to battle for that position, or do you want to start as left defensive end?"

Of course I wanted to start, so I stepped forward into the D-line.

When I'd first tried out for football in high school, I had wanted to play in the defensive line, but for the past few months, I'd been immersing myself in the linebacker's role. I could've done well as a linebacker. I had the size and speed, and I'd studied the position thoroughly, but the coaching staff had other plans.

This was my first glimpse into the behind-the-scenes maneuvering of college football. Decisions weren't based purely on love of the game because millions of dollars were at stake. Players had to joust for positions in order to make it to the next level, and the coaching staff had their own careers and families to consider. There was pressure to get TV and licensing deals and to satisfy high-donor alumni fans. In a word, college football involved politics.

So once again, I had to learn a new position. In high school, where I'd played offensive right guard, my main effort was to protect my quarterback and block tackles. As a defensive end, my job was just the reverse. I had to rush the opposing quarterback and tackle ball carriers. Instead of the linebacker's upright stance, I'd be taking the three-point stance, bending deeper at the waist, placing my right hand on the ground, with my left foot forward and right foot back, perched and ready to spring.

Summer practice took up three or four hours each day, and I became a "playbook junkie." I carried the playbook everywhere. The plays we practiced were more complex than what I'd known in high school. The playbook described each play, but reading text was not my optimal way to learn. I comprehended more by drawing diagrams as the coach described each play aloud. It also helped that the staff filmed our moves from every angle, and we discussed the footage together.

When we weren't practicing, we spent our free time playing pick-up basketball and endless video games. Summer sessions were called "May-mesters," because they ran May through July, and most athletes attended a few classes in order to get "summer school checks" from Vanderbilt financial aid. As a result, we had a little pocket money.

It was during the summer before sophomore year that Cheron and I cut each other's hair. Neither of us could afford the cost of maintaining our braids, so we got scissors and gave each other mullets, short at the front and sides and long in back. We laughed about it for a week, but then we went to a barber and got real haircuts.

That summer, I also got my first tattoo. I'd been thinking about it for some time, so one Friday afternoon, four of us went to the tattoo parlor together. I'd already decided that I would not pick a stock image from a book. Instead, I described the image I wanted, and the tattoo artist drew it.

Since my nickname was Jungle, I chose a jungle panther, my high school mascot. He's poised on a rock surrounded by jungle foliage, with a misty night sky in the background. There's an inscription, too. It reads, "Welcome to the Jungle," the title of a song by my favorite hard rock band, Guns and Roses.

It's a large tattoo, covering the deltoid muscle of my left shoulder. The dark panther and the dark night sky required a lot of inking, and halfway through the process, the needle hurt so much that I almost called a stop. But after it was done, I thought it was beautiful. I wanted to show everyone. The very next week, I got another.

These days, I've lost count of the tattoos ornamenting my body. I no longer show them off, because they're for me, not for others. Some people associate tattoos with gang members and thugs, but tattoos don't harm anyone. Neither does a pierced nose or a set of earlobe plugs. In my opinion, body ornaments are a form of personal expression.

When fall classes began, our 2-Trill group continued to party as much as ever, through the week and especially on Saturday nights. We stayed up till the wee hours, drinking and laughing, and sometimes we smoked weed. We were young and strong, and we felt immortal, believing our bodies could take any amount of abuse. I, for instance, was doing two-hour workouts twice a day. I ran laps, lifted weights, and did jumps. I pushed my knees and ankles to the limit. I felt powerful. Still it's true that heavy drinking and smoking affected me.

On Sunday mornings after a night of drinking, I'd feel terrible. I'd grab a quick breakfast and juice in our dormitory "Munchie Mart." Then all through the Sunday morning drills and workouts, I'd gasp and cough. When I couldn't get my breath, I thought, "This is killing me." But I didn't stop.

Sometimes I slept through classes, or sometimes I skipped them. Practice, workouts, learning the playbook and reviewing footage were more important – not to mention hanging out with 2-Trill. Though academics took a back burner, I did enough work to continue improving my grade point average. Mrs. Wright helped me identify classes that would fit my interests, like the History of Baseball. It was not an easy class, but it held my attention. I also enjoyed the History of Music, until we started listening to opera.

On the other hand, all the classes in Human and Organizational Development were engaging. My favorite professor was Dr. Brian Griffith, one of the finest professors at Vanderbilt. He taught us to study human behavior through observation. We'd do field trips around campus, observing people in the quads or in another class. We'd be graded on what we noticed. Once we went people-watching at the Vanderbilt Medical Center, and I found that fascinating.

Brian Griffith was about 5'10", medium build, with brown hair and glasses. He was a genuine guy, serious but not stern. In a classroom discussion about the choices people make, he told us about his brother who committed suicide, and by the end, everyone had wet eyes. He knew all his students, and if you were willing to work, he'd work with you. The events of 9/11 occurred while I was in his class, and he became as emotional as the rest of us.

Once he said to me, "I see the effort you put into football. If you worked that hard in academics, you could excel in your studies, too."

Later on, he assigned me a topic to present in his class, and I took it seriously. I decided not to read from PowerPoint slides, as I usually did. Instead, I wrote out my speech on note cards and memorized them. The speech ran twenty minutes, and my nerves were so jittery before class, I spent the entire morning reciting the speech in my head. By class time, my note cards were soggy with sweat.

Brian called my name, and I told myself, "I'm going to do this." Then I intentionally left my note cards in my seat. The class was large, and Brian sat in the front, listening and grading. As I walked down to the podium, my teammates watched with something like dread. They'd heard me stumble through presentations before, and they expected a repeat. But I intended to prove them wrong. For the first eight minutes, I was rolling. My delivery was letter perfect, and inside I was laughing.

About then, I glanced at Brian, and he gave me a thumbs-up. That was just enough to distract me. All at once, I could not remember the next line. I stood dumbfounded. My note cards were up in my seat. I couldn't think. As the pause lengthened, my teammates started to laugh.

Brian said, "Take a couple breaths. Then go through it in your head, and pick up where you left off."

My head was empty. Panic had swept away every thought.

Again Brian prodded me. "Just try."

I did the only thing I could. I turned and read the bullet points on my PowerPoint slides. Sweat roll down my face, and I repeatedly wiped it away with my hand. I might have given up if not for Brian. When I finished, the entire class applauded. Then Brian stood up and hugged me. "Man, I'm proud of you."

I thought I'd blown it. Another teacher would've given me a bad grade, but not Brian. That's the kind of guy he was.

CHAPTER TWENTY-FOUR

You Can't Think Straight Until The Hangover Passes

When football season started, we never partied the night before a game. I knew better than to risk that. Also, the team had curfew, and to make sure we stayed sober, the university put us up in hotel rooms, even for home games. I think most universities use that method to supervise their players.

In my opinion, the Southeastern Conference, or SEC, is the greatest conference in college football. Vanderbilt plays in the SEC, but that year we ranked near the bottom. At away games, we played in massive stadiums full of frenzied fans cheering for our opponents. Georgia, South Carolina, Florida, their crowds exploded in ecstasy every time we lost possession of the ball. The University of Tennessee, our biggest rival, had the largest stadium and the most passionate fans. Even at our own home games, the UT fans outnumbered ours. When we played LSU, Louisiana fans threw rocks at our team bus and tried to tip us over. I saw a five-year-old giving us the finger. That chilled me.

Right before we played Georgia, our team bus got hit by an eighteen-wheeler truck in a freak highway accident. The impact caved in one whole side of our bus, and only minutes before, I'd been asleep on that side with my head against the window. If I hadn't moved, I would've been decapitated. Remarkably, nobody died, but several people were cut up and bleeding. We had legitimate grounds to cancel our game, but when coach asked if we still wanted to play, we said yes. The trauma left us unable to concentrate, though, and once again we lost.

The day we played the University of Florida was hot and muggy, the stadium was packed, and we were getting killed. Florida's band was playing the shark theme from the movie *Jaws,* and their fans were doing the "Gator Chomp," using their outstretched arms to simulate an alligator's mouth opening and closing. They swayed back and forth like moving water. When they did the Wave, their roar was like a roller-coaster going over us. Cheron, Dominique, Moses, Kelechi and I were standing together on the field. We looked at each other, and Cheron said, "This is real college football."

That season, Vanderbilt won only two games, neither of them against SEC teams. The losing streak sapped everyone's enthusiasm, including mine. I suppose we gave our fans good reason not to care.

The regular college football season runs for sixteen weeks, from late August through December. Next come the bowl games, in which Vanderbilt rarely plays. That year was no exception. The night before our final practice in December, 2002, we cast secret ballots for the three team captains who would lead us the following season. Then in March, 2003, Vanderbilt staged an intra-squad football match called the Spring Game, just before the start of summer training. As part of the event, they hosted a large cookout for the team, families and fans. About four hundred people attended, and that's when they announced the names of our three captains.

When they announced my name, my jaw dropped. I had zero inkling my teammates would choose me for that honor. I'd played only one year, and being voted captain had never crossed my mind. "El Capitan," my friends joked, patting me on the back.

When the Coach called me to the middle of the field, I was in a state of dismay. I stood with the two other captains, Jay Cutler and Justin Geisinger, while the media took our pictures and asked questions. "What do you expect for the upcoming season, Jovan?"

"The best," I answered.

Shortly after that, Vanderbilt staged its annual music festival called the Rites of Spring, and over twenty bands were scheduled to play. The headliner was Nappy Roots, the most popular hip hop band in America at that time. The party began Friday night and ran through Saturday, and Cheron and I decided to make it epic.

Our Friday night party was crazy, and on Saturday, my plan was to drink a different alcoholic beverage every hour. I started at 9:00 am with a couple of shots of vodka. Then I moved to rum, then beer. I'm not sure what came next. I remember going back to my room at 8:00 pm, downing a plastic cupful of straight vodka, then staggering back outside.

Nappy Roots was performing on the lawn, and thousands of students, friends and families sat in the grass listening. Suddenly I realized that, despite the band's enormous speakers, I couldn't hear one word of what they were singing. I wandered up to the stage to hear better. Then I spotted a friend with an open bottle of Bacardi, and when he wasn't looking, I grabbed it and ran. He chased me, yelling and cursing, while I drank the whole bottle. That was my last memory.

I woke up in my room, face down on the carpet. Cheron was tapping me, saying, "Jovan, you okay?"

When I sat up, the worst headache of my life pounded through my skull. Cheron called some 2-Trill friends into my room, and gradually they told me what had happened the previous night. They said I harassed some stranger, then roamed around campus overturning Port-o-Johns. The campus police held me briefly, concerned that I might have alcohol poisoning. After they let me go, I sat on the front porch crying to a campus worker that I didn't know who I was anymore.

As my friends told me these stories, I sat with my head in my hands, unable to make sense of what they were saying. The alcohol had wiped my memory and left me physically ill.

Later, other friends told me more. One girl said, "I never saw anyone cry like that. You scared me to death."

I felt mortified. All day, my skull throbbed, and every new detail added to my shame. I wanted to bury my head under my pillow. Only after the hangover passed was I able to think straight, and one fact became clear. I was on the wrong path. My behavior had to change.

As horrible as that experience had been, it spurred me to make one of the wisest decisions of my life. From that day to this, I have not smoked tobacco or weed or touched another drop of alcohol – except once. Years later at a friend's New Year's Eve party, I took a sip of champagne, and the instant it hit my tongue, I felt woozy. Whether my reaction was physical or psychosomatic doesn't matter. I set the glass down and didn't finish it. Ridding my body of chemicals made me stronger, more alert and better prepared to play the game I loved. In my heart, I vowed that my next season of football would be outstanding.

CHAPTER TWENTY-FIVE

The Two Things We Control In The Game Are Our Attitude And Effort

In July before my junior – or redshirt sophomore – year, Coach Johnson chose the three team captains to represent the Vanderbilt Commodores at "SEC Media Days," a three-day sports media circus in Hoover, Alabama, near Birmingham. For the annual event, each of the twelve SEC head coaches selects three players to represent the team at a scheduled press conference, and hundreds of sports reporters and camera crews attend. The event is broadcast live on ESPN, and scores of fans swarm the hotel lobbies.

Money was still tight for me, so I went to a discount store to buy a gray plaid jacket, a pair of black trousers and a tie. Coach said we had to be clean-cut, so I shaved off my beard, and that was not a good look for me. The award for "Best Dressed" would not come my way.

At our press conference, we mounted a stage in a large hotel meeting room, and the reporters started firing questions. Our season had not been stellar, and some of our answers were awkward. There were long pauses. Later, we had to give radio interviews. I enjoyed talking about football, but I was glad when the event was finally over. For the rest of that summer, I stayed on campus, practicing, working out, and taking classes to earn my "summer school checks."

That year, Dad saved up enough money to buy me a 1995 Nissan Maxima, white with peanut-butter interior. I was the happiest person alive. Sometimes I'd drive around campus just to show off my new car. Other Vandy kids had BMWs and Mercedes, but I was proud of my Nissan. Also, Cheron and I became roommates. He was witty and fun to be with, a real friend. Though I continued to hang out with 2-Trill and attend frat parties, I didn't drink anymore, and my behavior was much more reserved. Instead of dancing and cutting loose, I simply talked to people. I've always been a talker.

I still exhibited many symptoms of attention deficit hyperactive disorder, or ADHD. Perhaps the worst was that if a topic didn't interest me, it simply would not hold my attention. Forcing myself to study such a topic was like trying to push a piece of cooked spaghetti through the eye of a needle. It didn't help that football consumed the majority of my physical and mental energy.

Grades were important at Vanderbilt, and for many students, a B+ meant the end of the world. One year, a pre-med student jumped off a multi-story parking garage onto a concrete sidewalk because he failed to get into grad school. In such a high-pressure environment, you can imagine how my classmates viewed my C-grade performance. On the rare occasions when an assignment actually interested me, I did well. For instance, we had to give a presentation about our chosen profession, and I spoke about pro football, a topic I thoroughly understood. That speech earned me an A, and when I showed my grade to some other students, they looked at me as if I'd cheated.

After one especially poor presentation, a professor called me aside and said, "Why are you here, Jovan? Did you come to learn or just to play football?"

I gave his question careful thought. "To be honest," I said, "football comes first. I just need this class in order to play."

He shook his head as if I'd given the wrong answer. "At the rate you're going, you'll fail," he said.

I said, "That's not an option. What do I have to do?"

"Don't expect any favors," he said. "Show some kind of effort."

I tried. I made myself listen in his class and jot down the other students' ideas. When called on to speak or to write an essay, I repeated what I'd heard, though it was pretty obvious the ideas were not my own. I earned a low grade in that class, but at least I didn't fail.

In another class, we were assigned to do a group presentation on a famous figure. I was sitting in the back row with two other football players, Kelechi and a guy named Ralph, and as the class broke into groups, people scattered away from us as if we carried plague.

We just looked at each other, and I said, "I guess we're the group."

Kelechi was furious, though. He made straight A's, and he didn't deserve that kind of treatment. Ralph was a good student, too. Ralph said, "You see how they disrespect us?"

"We'll do the best presentation in class," Kelechi said. "We're going to show those bleep bleep guys."

"Yeah, let's do this," I said.

That same night, Kelechi called us together to plan. "Let's dig in," he said.

For our famous figure, we chose Tupac Shakur, the internationally known rapper and actor. I didn't know much about Tupac, but the more I learned, the more absorbed I became. Not only did we research his life and work, we also studied his poetry and read books he'd read, trying to get deeper into his mind. Tupac's parents were members of the Black Panthers, and his songs were full of the violence and vulgar language of inner city ghettos. He was often associated with gangsters and shootings, and as everyone knows, he himself was shot to death after a street brawl. But we wanted to get past that and see the real man.

On the day of our presentation, we came to class in costume. Ralph came as Suge Knight, the owner of Tupac's music label, Death Row Records. Kelechi came as Tupac, and I came dressed as his bodyguard. We played video and music clips, and we put on two skits about his life. As our presentation unfolded, I noticed the looks on people's faces. They were whispering, "Wow, these guys are doing great."

Our presentation got the highest grade, and that was one of the proudest moments of my academic career. My most serious study, though, remained football. By this point, I was watching game film three or four hours a day. When I watched games on TV, I could no longer view them as a fan. I was constantly analyzing and making mental notes. Watching ESPN was work.

Not only did I learn our playbook by heart. I also learn the role of every position on the D-line. The minute Coach introduced a new play on the board, I got it. I knew how to read an opposing team's formation and how each defensive player should respond. If one of my teammates forgot, I would be there to remind him. That made it easier for me to help the younger guys, and in time I became a sort of natural leader.

During the game, everything moves at tremendous speed, and you can't be thinking and analyzing while the bullets are flying. You have to know in advance what to do. If dyslexia brought me a blessing, it was the habit of preparing ahead. Coaches will tell you they'd rather have a good player making the right play than a world-class athlete who's out of step.

David Turner, our D-line coach, said, "There are only two things you can control in the game, your attitude and your effort."

I took his words to heart. Besides studying film and training my body, I made it a point of honor to let everyone know how happy I was to be there, playing the game I loved. As a result, my teammates began to feed off my energy. I encouraged them, and I also pushed them. During workouts, for instance, if a guy wasn't investing enough, I'd call him on it.

As team captain, I took pride in mentoring the younger guys and teaching them everything I'd learned. Whereas some players worry that younger men may outshine them, it's my belief that sharing knowledge makes the whole team better. If someone outperforms me, that's how it's meant to be.

I've been on the other side, young and hungering to learn, while the older guys didn't care to help. Now I feel that if I'm not helping other players to the best of my ability, then what's the point of the team? "God don't like ugly," my Auntie Dell used to say. She meant we should follow the Golden Rule.

My performance that year was everything I'd hoped for. I knew my opponents. I knew their strengths and weaknesses, their habits and tendencies. I knew how to slow the plays down in my head and focus on winning the game within the game, the individual battle with the man facing me across the scrimmage line. I'd grown bigger, stronger and more confident. My teammates had grown stronger, too, and many besides me were achieving individual success.

The high point came when we beat the University of Kentucky Wildcats, our first win against an SEC team in twenty years. I remember it was dreary and overcast that day, and the Vanderbilt Stadium lights were shining. When we won, our fans rushed onto the field and tore down both goal posts. After being at the bottom so long, this was transformative. Virtually the entire student body partied that night, and a mob of students carried one of the goal posts all the way from our stadium to Riverfront Park in downtown Nashville. Their parade blocked traffic, yet the police stood by smiling and waving them on. The next day at our team meeting, Coach Johnson gave us each a piece of iron cut from the goal post.

That year, I made First Team All-SEC and Third Team Preseason All-American. Many commentators regarded me as one of the top three players in the SEC, along with Marcus Spears of LSU and David Pollack of Georgia. I looked up to both those guys, and it was a huge honor to have my name mentioned with theirs.

Despite my performance, Vanderbilt won only two games all season, and for me, losing was the worst. In some games, I knew in my soul that I'd played the best football of my career, and still we lost. That sickened me. Once, we were riding on the team bus after a loss, and I felt torn up inside. In the back rows, some of my teammates were joking and laughing. They hadn't expected to win, and that tormented me. Tears were streaming down my cheeks. I stood up and yelled at them to take the game more seriously.

Many times, I thought of leaving Vanderbilt early to enter the NFL draft. By this time, it was clear that I had a legitimate shot. In preparation, I began loading up on classes so that if I did leave early, I could still graduate. The degree was important to me, but my real professional career would be football.

At year's end, my final grade point average stood at 2.3, a modest C+. I felt pleased with that grade, but to my surprise, Cheron raised his average to a solid B, which qualified him for the All SEC honor roll.

"How'd you do that?" I asked.

"I went to class and paid attention," he said. "I studied with my girlfriend while you were watching ESPN."

Cheron had snuck one past me. So had other 2-Trillers, it turned out. I'd been wrong to assume they were as obsessed with football as I was.

CHAPTER TWENTY-SIX

If You're Gasping For Breath, Don't Bend Over. The Air Is Up Top

Once again, the team elected me as one of the three captains, and that July, when we returned to the "SEC Media Days," everything was different. Though we'd had a losing season, my performance had earned accolades, and our press conference was packed. Reporters peppered me with questions about my personal success, and for once, I could answer with pride. Also, I'd taken note of the dress code the year before. A lot of players wore colorful suits and ruffled shirts, as if they were going to a prom. So I came decked out in a swank peach-and-cream tuxedo. That year, I won "Best Dressed" by a landslide.

By now, I thought my dyslexia was a thing of the past. I could speak clearly, and the work-around techniques I'd developed for reading and math continued to serve me. My grade point average had been rising each year. But I was wrong about dyslexia. Another one of its many complication was about to surface, this time on the football field.

This fourth year at Vanderbilt marked my third season of college football, my redshirt junior year, and after my strong performance the year before, everyone expected big things from me. In fact, the general feeling was that if I entered the NFL draft, I'd be picked late in the second round, at worst. That's probably why Coach Johnson changed my task and gave me more responsibility. Instead of playing defensive left end, he assigned me to play a versatile role, always facing the opponent's tight end.

The first inkling that this would give me trouble came when I tried to reverse my stance to play on the right end. On the left end, my stance was low and strong, right hand forward in the dirt, right leg back. All my power came from my right side, and from that stance, I could move like a bolt. But the tight end's hybrid role as both offensive blocker and wide receiver meant his position would change from play to play, and I had to face him no matter where he lined up. So I had to learn a mirror-image stance, placing my left hand in the dirt and pushing off from my left foot. This was like Delilah cutting Samson's hair. Suddenly, I had no strength at all.

From the very first moment, this reverse stance felt awkward. All the steps were backward. I had to kick off on the wrong foot, then turn to get going. It threw my timing off. I couldn't operate that way. I'd always been very right-hand dominant, and even today, for instance, if I'm driving and changing lanes, I can't simply glance over my left shoulder to check my blind spot. I have to twist around and look with my right eye, although the vision in my left eye is perfect.

Researchers have now learned that extreme "handedness" is yet another facet of dyslexia. According to a study conducted at the University of Oxford in England, a genetic mutation causes asymmetrical development of the brain, which is linked to both extreme handedness and the reading disorders associated with dyslexia. That final year at Vandy, though, I just felt baffled.

In the end, I had to stick with my stronger right-foot stance, no matter where I played on the scrimmage line. That slowed me down, but I'd always been a role guy, willing to do whatever the team needed. Even then, I still expected to have a great year. Coach wasn't worried about my personal success. He just wanted to win, and that's what I wanted, too.

During workouts and practice, I turned up the intensity, demanding more from teammates as well as myself. Coach told us, "If you're gasping for breath, don't bend over. Remember the air is up top." That was his way of telling us to show strength, no matter how we felt.

Many times, my insides would be literally burning, yet the entire time I played for Vanderbilt, I never once bent over. I expected no less from my teammates, because a paramount rule of football is always to show strength, never weakness. Frankly, I pushed everyone too hard at times. Some guys became dizzy or nauseous during long workouts, and when I treated that as a sign of weakness, they got mad.

Later, I had to change my attitude about weakness. After I heard of cases where student athletes dropped dead from heart attack or passed out from heat stroke during a hot summer practice, I scaled back the pressure. Anytime a player claimed sickness, I let the team doctor take care of him. Personally, I could fight through cramps, exhaustion and pain, but I couldn't judge for others.

On game days, when our team stayed together in a hotel, we'd have brunch with the coaching staff in a private banquet hall. After the coaches left, we'd have our own pre-game speeches. All three captains spoke, and other players sometimes spoke as well. My speeches were the most passionate.

My job was to stir the guys up and make them feel the love of the game. Too many of our players expected to lose, so I used a combination of encouragement and threats. Losing gave me real physical pain, and more than once I got so frustrated about our team's attitude that I smashed a dinner plate. The first time I did that, the guys were shocked. Another time, in an outburst of passion, I flipped a table over.

"This is our chance to make something of ourselves!" I yelled. "Today's the day we get this done. If you're not ready to give everything, don't even come to the game!"

As the season wore on and we continued to lose, there were nights when I didn't bother to say anything. I simply stood up, looked everybody in the eye, then turned and left. They knew what I meant.

In all my years at Vanderbilt, we never won more than two games a season, and we never made it to a bowl game. My redshirt junior year was no exception. Though I did my best in my new assignment, I did not achieve the numbers everyone expected. Did I feel bitter that Coach had changed my role? It's true my NFL career might have gone a different way if I'd had a second stellar year at Vanderbilt. But no, I'm not angry. The change helped me learn a lot more about the game of football.

My varying position forced me to develop new skills in hand placement and controlling and shedding blockers. I also became much better at stopping runs. Before, I'd focused on rushing passes, but in my new role, I developed a love for defending against runs. By studying film and keying in on my opponents' tendencies, I learned to recognize and respond to running plays faster. This helped me later in the pros. Some D-line players specialize in only one kind of play, runs or passes, but for the rest of my career, I was able to handle both.

Nevertheless, losing takes a toll on the psyche. As the season wound down, I began to think seriously about leaving Vanderbilt early to enter the NFL draft. I lacked only seven hours of course work, so I'd have no problem finishing my degree in the off season. But it wasn't an easy decision. There were risks.

For one thing, I could enter the draft and potentially not be picked at all. That would be a disaster for my career. My scholarship covered another full year at Vanderbilt, but once I entered the draft, the rules prohibited me from ever again playing college football, so my scholarship would end. Entering the draft early would be a major gamble.

For weeks, I discussed the pros and cons with my friends, until I finally made up my mind. Another year in college might have benefited me, but I simply could not stand to keep losing. Every defeat demoralized me, and the idea of facing the firing squad at SEC Media Days made me ill. So after our final loss to UT, I went to see Coach Johnson. I thanked him for everything he'd done and told him what I'd decided.

"Wait, let's discuss this," he said. "Have you talked to your parents?"

I just shook my head and told him my mind was made up.

In December, 2004, I left Vanderbilt, and the following April, I entered the NFL draft. Looking back, I have no regrets about choosing Vanderbilt. While I was there, I started 34 of 35 games and recorded 149 tackles, 10.5 sacks, and one interception. Of course I wish we'd won more games, but I still love the school and cheer for the Commodores. If I'd gone to a stronger football university, the competition would have been stiffer, and I might not have played as much. As far as academics, I would have struggled no matter which college I attended. Though I'm proud of my degree, football was always my chosen career.

What I do regret was that I tried to be someone I was not. I tried to be a party guy, and that's not who I am.

Before starting college, I had promised myself not to smoke or drink, and I regret breaking that promise. Still, the experience taught me a lesson about what kind of adult I wanted to be. For that, I'm grateful.

Vanderbilt gave me a magnificent gift – a springboard into the surreal world of the NFL, where a top player's annual salary can exceed what another professional might hope to earn in a lifetime. Pro football is a fantasy job, and every day I wake up knowing I've been blessed. Doctors and lawyers may have careers spanning thirty or forty years, but football players never last that long. We experience a brief exhilaration. Then it's over. I never wanted anything else.

CHAPTER TWENTY-SEVEN

Every Day, I Look At The Number Tattooed On My Arm

The NFL Annual Player Selection Meeting, better known as the NFL draft, is held each year on an April weekend midway between the Super Bowl and the start of training camp in July. Millions of fans watch on TV as all thirty-two NFL teams take turns drafting young, mostly college level players, although any player who's been out of high school at least three years can enter the draft, simply by declaring his eligibility in January.

There are seven rounds of picks, and each team usually has one pick per round, unless they trade their picks. The team with the worst record gets first pick in each round, and the best performing team gets last pick. The round in which a player is picked is crucial because it determines how much money he'll make, and it's one of the key stats that follows him throughout his career. However, many players are never picked. Only one in fifty college football seniors get picked in the NFL draft.

My first step, after declaring my eligibility in January, 2005, was to choose an agent. My one outstanding college season put me in high favor, and some projections showed that I would be picked in one of the first three rounds. Agents were eager to represent me, and several called to offer their services. I settled on Jack Sharf, an experienced and well-connected agent with Momentum Sports.

Jack already represented seven pro players, and he made me feel confident. He looked like a Wall Street banker in his suit and slick hairstyle. He had a straightforward, no-nonsense manner, and he knew his business. Jack told me that if I trained hard before the draft, I could raise my stock even further.

Long before the draft began, scouts, coaches and general managers were already assessing top college players, and a few coaches and scouts would attend Vanderbilt's "Pro Day" to watch our team perform. More important would be the NFL Scouting Combine, held weeks before college "Pro Days." The Combine was an invitation-only showcase for top players. While only a small number of scouts would see Vandy's Pro Day, every NFL team would send scouts to the Combine. When Jack called to say I'd been invited, I felt tremendous relief. The Combine would let me show what I could do in front of everyone.

To prepare for the Combine, Jack sent me to Athletes' Performance in Tempe, Arizona, a famous training center for professional athletes. Many All-Americans rely on this world-class center. Thank goodness Jack's agency fronted the funds for my training because I could not have afforded the $30,000 fee.

The Tempe facility was top-of-the-line, with the latest equipment, hot and cold tubs, massages, chiropractic services, and more. They fed us tasty well-balanced meals, monitored our health, customized our workouts, and even coached us in giving interviews. I took advantage of everything they offered. Every day I worked out at fullest capacity, all through the early weeks of 2005, right up till just before the draft in late April. I was determined to build my strength, speed, flexibility and endurance. Plus, I also received another kind of training – for my mind.

Twice each week, I met with a counselor, one on one. He helped me pick apart my attitude and strengthen my focus. In a darkened room, he led me in yoga meditation to teach me how to clear my head before a game and visualize my achievement on the field, step by step. "You have to win up top," he told me. At first, I didn't take his idea seriously, but when I saw what a difference it made in my performance, I realized that winning the mental game was the core of success.

My time at Athletes' Performance was a beautiful experience. Although the workouts were grueling, I finished in the best shape of my life. At 6'2", I weighed 285 pounds with only 7 percent body fat. In other words, I was ripped.

Not every day was sunny though. One January morning around 3:00 am, a phone call woke me up. It was Cheron calling to say a teammate of ours had been shot and killed.

Kwanye Doster. We called him Dot. He had gone home to Tampa, Florida to visit his family, and he was eating in the back seat of a friend's car when the ordeal took place. Dot reached down to take a bite, and the stranger must have thought he was reaching for a gun. Dot took a direct blast to his upper body. The worst part was, Dot was just in the wrong place at the wrong time. He died too young.

Kwanye Doster was a good man whose thuggish exterior masked a gentle spirit. He loved to joke, and I rarely ever saw him get mad. He played running back, and we all thought he was on his way to the NFL. I remember his reason for playing football was to take care of his family, especially his little brother who followed him around like a shadow. He used to describe his Tampa neighborhood as a war zone. He was killed on Sunday. I got the call Monday morning, and that same day, I flew to Nashville to catch the Vanderbilt team plane to Tampa. Our whole team attended Dot's funeral.

At the service, my teammates and I cried more than Dot's relatives, but I think I understand why. In neighborhoods like the ones where Dot and I grew up, too many worthy young people die in street violence, and after a while, relatives get numb. That was my first confrontation with murder, and I pray it will be the last. My flight back to Tempe after the service was clouded in sadness.

It was after I returned to Athletes' Performance that staff doctors first diagnosed my high blood pressure. During extreme workouts, I sometimes felt the room start to spin, and my blood pressure reading would shoot up to 170/135.

Medications brought this condition under control, and it has remained under control ever since, but as the Combine approached, I wanted to make doubly sure, so I drank raw garlic juice for a week.

Each February, the NFL Scouting Combine convenes in Indianapolis, Indiana. It runs Friday through Sunday, so on the Thursday before, I flew from warm sunny Arizona into dreary Indiana snow. Being invited to the Combine was a great privilege, but I did not enjoy the experience. It felt like a meat market.

The first day involved physical exams, and seven different team doctors examined me, looking for past injuries and potential problems. I endured multiple X-rays and an MRI. They ran blood work and drug screenings, tugged on my joints, asked what medications I was taking. My shoulder injury had healed, but they were curious how I had gained 50 pounds of muscle mass between my redshirt freshman and sophomore years. They asked if I'd taken steroids, but I assured them I had not. I'd simply been eating right and doing intense daily work-outs. I later learned the 50-pound weight gain in my record was probably a typo.

On the second day, we had to strip down to tights and march across a stage. They measured our height, chest, arm span and hand span. My height measured a couple of inches shorter than the average D-lineman, but I had the widest arm and hand span of anyone there. Next the strength and position coaches watched us do bench presses. I pressed 35 reps at 225 pounds.

Later that day, I had to take the Wonderlic Cognitive Ability Test, a timed test that gauges your learning and problem-solving aptitude. Timed tests had always been my enemy, yet I didn't dare reveal that I had dyslexia. At the Combine, any little drawback can knock you out of the running. So I took the test in silence, and no surprise, I scored low.

At night, we had meetings with team representatives. I had seven scheduled meetings that weekend, and also a few quick unscheduled ones. During these meetings, the scouts, coaches and general managers grilled me about my upbringing, my family situation, my involvement with drugs, violence, and so on. They were looking for any snag that might affect how I played football, and they already knew the answers before I spoke. They'd run detailed background checks and studied my film. Some of them asked me again about steroids. I answered every question with the simple truth. Drafting a new player is a major investment, so I understood their rigorous due diligence. Still, those meetings wore me out.

On the third day, we each ran a 40-yard dash, made broad jumps and vertical high jumps, then performed short and long shuffle runs around cones. Next, in alphabetical order, we took turns doing field drills. My numbers were off the chart. For my size and position, I jumped the highest, ran the fastest and lifted the most weight of anyone.

After that, everybody was slapping my back, saying "Wow, man!" My agent was laying bets that I would be picked in the first round. In a few early mock drafts, I was designated to be picked "late first round, no later than third." When I left Indiana, I was soaring.

Vandy's Pro Day was held a couple of weeks before the draft, but the drills were hand-timed with a stopwatch, not digitally measured. So I "sat on my numbers" from the Combine. Already, I was getting calls from investment advisors and lenders offering cash advances against my signing bonus. Everyone expected me to strike gold. Nothing could slow me down.

The 2005 draft was held on April 23 and 24 at the Jacob K. Javits Convention Center in New York. I flew to Florida to watch it on TV with my parents and brother. The Sunshine Network wanted to run a live "Draft Special" on me, shot in our living room with a mobile broadcast truck parked out front. But I didn't want cameras. What if I didn't get picked? My agent pushed me to do it, but I said no. I'm glad of that decision.

There are seven rounds in the draft, and with each passing round, the amount of money a player can expect to earn drops fast. For me, though, the draft was more about being recognized and getting a chance to play with a great team. My hope was to be picked no later than the second round.

On Saturday, we watched the first three rounds go by without my name being called. I'm grateful my disappointment was not broadcast on live TV. Only fifteen defensive ends were drafted that year, and at last, on Sunday, April 24, 2006, I was chosen in the sixth round by the Carolina Panthers. Of the 255 total players drafted, I was pick 189.

Why did it go that way? The steroid rumor? My low Wonderlic score? My below-average height? I'll never know the reason. Each team has its own criteria for picking players, and few of us can guess what factors influence the management decisions made "upstairs." After dominating the Combine, my late draft pick came as a blow. That statistic would stay with me forever, so I went out and had the number "189" tattooed on my arm. Every day, I looked at the permanent record inscribed on my skin, and the sight of it motivated me to keep trying harder.

CHAPTER TWENTY-EIGHT

Getting Your Wish Is Only The Beginning

In 2005, the Carolina Panthers possessed arguably the best defensive line in the NFL. With top All-Americans and Pro Bowlers, they were loaded with talent all across the D-line. When they first drafted me, I didn't pay attention to that. All I knew was that they'd given me a chance to live my dream. Only later did I realize how little they needed a new defensive end and how slim were my chances of getting on the field. In my rookie season, I was "on the bubble," as they say. Whether I would make the cut or be cut was a toss-up.

I didn't know any of that when I flew to Charlotte, North Carolina, one day after the draft. I felt both on top of the world and racked by anxiety. I'd become a member of the National Football League, the most exalted American football league in the world. It's scary when such a big dream comes true. That's when you recognize that getting your wish is only the beginning.

First-round draft picks get flights on chartered jets, but I took a commercial airline. No flashing cameras met me at the airport, only a scout who drove me to a hotel. Other draft picks and free agents were idling in the lobby when we arrived. We'd come for a "mini-camp" for rookies. I passed the evening as well as I could, but it seemed like a billion thoughts were racing through my mind. When my alarm went off early the next morning, I was tied up in knots.

I dressed in flip-flops, black shorts and white tee-shirt, then grabbed my backpack and went to catch the van with the other players. There were about thirty rookies altogether. We drove to the facility for breakfast, then dressed for practice and took a short tour.

The Panthers' training facility was located on the same site as the stadium. Management offices were upstairs, but the cafeteria, weight room, players' lounge and locker room were all on the same level as the stadium field. After visiting several facilities, I liked the Panthers' arrangement best because we could keep all our gear in the same locker for both practices and games.

An attractive walking path linked the facility to our three practice fields, and although the grounds were gated, fenced, and guarded, fans would often line up along the fences to watch us practice. That worried me at first because I felt exposed to possible drive-by shootings.

My imagination always seemed to jump to the worst possible scenarios, but soon enough, I began to relax.

That first morning at the facility, I saw three star veterans working out – defensive end Julius Peppers, wide receiver Steve Smith, and nose tackle Kris Jenkins. I knew right then I was in heady company. After the tour, we met with Head Coach John "Foxy" Fox for about half an hour. Coach Fox had a cool exterior, but he was a player's coach. He took care of his players, and his guys respected him. The whole time I played for him, though, he never got my name right. He called me Jonathan, which I found funny.

After meeting Coach Fox, we broke up into individual team meetings. In our defensive meeting, I received two thick playbooks, one for defense and one for special teams. It takes an exceptional guy to play special teams. These players handle kick-offs, punts, extra point kicks, field goal kicks, and other special actions. They have more plays to learn, longer practices, and fewer breaks during a game. I tip my hat to special team guys, but I didn't want to join them. At Vanderbilt, I'd been spoiled. In Carolina, by contrast, I was assigned to all special teams.

At our defensive team meeting, the coach began to introduce the plays. Then we went out on the field, walked through some plays and did individual drills. For the next two and a half days, we drilled and worked out twice daily and continued learning more plays. Practices were designed to simulate what real training camp would be like, so as you can imagine, they were intense. But I was in great shape, so I did well on the field.

Learning the playbook was not as easy. Professional playbooks are much more complex than college ball, and reading text and symbols on a page was never easy for me. I really struggled, yet I couldn't afford to ask for extra help because I had dyslexia. That might have been the kiss of death for my budding career. So instead, I spent extra hours of study on my own.

After the mini-camp and a brief visit to Ft. Lauderdale, I moved into the Holiday Inn in downtown Charlotte for a long summer of off-season workouts. In July, training camp began in Spartanburg, South Carolina, one of the hottest places in the U.S. We drilled daily for four weeks straight with only three days off. It was the most grueling camp I'd ever experienced.

By the end of camp, I'd learned more about the unforgiving nature of professional football. A single mistake on the field might cost my job, and I still hadn't mastered the Panthers' two-hundred-plus defensive plays, each with its own adjustments and audibles. However, each day's practice followed a script, and the staff posted a chart each morning, listing the plays we'd go through. So every day, I looked at the chart ahead of time and focused on memorizing just those plays.

One day, for instance, the script had us running six defensive plays in a row. I looked at my coach's chart and learned all six by heart. The first two plays went fine. I knew exactly where to be and what to do. But on the third play, the coach switched up the defensive call, and I was lost. On the fifth play, we went back to the script, but I was still shaken by my earlier mistake, and my mind went blank. Anxiety ruled. I couldn't think. Finally on the sixth play, I got my mind back in gear.

In our meeting afterward, all my mistakes were caught on film, and the coach called me out in front of everyone. Others had messed up, too, even some of the veterans. I wasn't alone. But seeing my mistakes on film made me ache inside, and I promised myself that I would do better. Looking back, it seems incredible that, by the end of training camp, I actually made "the 53," the total number of players allowed on an NFL team.

I also learned that NFL rookies go through hazing just like new fraternity brothers. Every team has its own traditions, from weird haircuts to ice baths. In the Carolina Panthers, the rookies have to serve the veterans like body slaves, carrying their gear, running their errands, and buying their breakfast and/or lunch every day of the season.

One veteran had an oversized ego, and he made things especially difficult. Once, he made me run to three different restaurants to pick up various parts of his lunch, and when I delivered the food, he made me take it back and get something else. Another rookie had to bring this same guy a box of Crackerjacks just before the team left for an away game, with a receipt time-stamped no more than one hour earlier, to show the box was freshly bought.

Another part of the Panthers' hazing tradition was the "Rookie Dinner." Our defensive line had three rookies, Lorenzo Alexander, Atiyyah Ellison, and me. For our dinner, we had to treat the entire D-line to a fancy meal at Bentley's, one of the finest restaurants in Charlotte. Our evening started with cold fresh-squeezed orange juice. Only God can make orange juice taste that good, and I drank many glasses at $4 each. But that was nothing compared to the multiple rounds of Louis XIII cognac some guys ordered at $250 a shot. We ordered the best of everything, and the food kept coming. We had a blast – until the check arrived. The total was $26,000.

We knew it would be a lot, but that seemed over the top, so we examined the bill. That's when we realized the guy with the oversized ego had ordered $13,000 in liquor, stashed it in his limo and left early. He had single-handedly doubled our bill.

Lorenzo, Atiyyah, and I pooled our funds, and we managed to come up with $19,000 between us. I had to call my credit card company to get an advance. Then three veterans, Julius Peppers, Mike Rucker and Al Wallace, stepped up to pay the rest, plus the tip. These guys were multi-millionaires, but they didn't let money inflate their egos. They were good guys, and I'll always be grateful for their generosity.

After training camp, I felt secure enough to move from my temporary Holiday Inn quarters to a more permanent residence. I leased a condo near the University of North Carolina at Charlotte, just across the hall from a team mate named Efrem Hill. We ate together, went to movies and clubs, had good times. As the 2005 season started, I began to feel less alone.

For the next seventeen weeks, the Panthers played almost every weekend, and I sat on the bench. I traveled to away games and stayed with the team at the hotel before home games. My name was on the roster, and every game day, I waited for Coach Fox to give me a thumbs up or down on whether I would dress to play. Thumbs down was disappointing, but it also meant relief. On those days, I could eat a big breakfast, four or five steaks with pancakes on the side.

Only twice in 2005 did I dress in full pads, and only once did I actually get on the field. We were facing the Green Bay Packers on Monday Night Football, and I felt as if the whole universe was watching. On my very first play, Packers quarterback Brett Favre threw a pass that whistled by my ear. It was a touchdown pass, and it seemed like the loudest sound I'd ever heard.

That year, the Carolina Panthers played against the Seattle Seahawks for the National Football Conference Championship. But our star defensive end, Julius Peppers, had a shoulder injury, and our team was fatigued from playing on the road four weeks straight. Although we lost 34 to 14, for me it was a thrill just to be there, watching from the bench.

Rookie years are a time for learning, and along with the Panthers' playbook, I also learned a lesson about money. That year marked the first time I had ever earned a pay check, and having money in my pocket was sweet. I got a $77,000 signing bonus, and my salary for the first year was $235,000, based on a $1.1 million four-year contract. I'd never had money like that, so I made up for lost time. I bought fine leather shoes, went to expensive restaurants, bought an SUV. My Yukon Denali XL was tricked out with all the extras, and it cost me $40,000. I also sent money home to my parents. I wanted to buy them a house and a car, but I didn't have enough for that yet.

As an NFL player, I was welcomed at elegant parties and clubs, and I met a lot of classy women. On Fridays after practice, I would get a haircut, then go home, shower and dress to go out. I didn't have a steady girlfriend, but I enjoyed taking women to movies and restaurants. The best advice I got about women came from the Panthers' defensive coordinator "Turg" Turgaloo. I'd become friends with linebacker Thomas Davis, a first-round draft pick who made a lot more money than me. Coach Turgaloo said, "If you get a girlfriend, don't let her hang out with Thomas's girl because you don't have Thomas's money." He went on to explain that my girl would be disappointed if I could not buy her what Thomas's girl had. The idea that women might be after my money had not registered before, so I thanked him for the advice.

But an even harder lesson about money lay in waiting. In May after my rookie year, I returned to Vanderbilt to finish my coursework and earn my degree. Soon after arriving, I invited about twenty friends to be my guests at Chili's, our old hangout. We had a royal evening, and I felt really happy to see my old friends. But when the time came to pay the bill, the waiter whispered, "Sorry sir, your credit card has been declined."

"No way," I said. "Can you run it through again?"

"Of course."

But when the waiter came back, he brought the same answer. Kelechi overheard and asked if he could help. I just laughed it off and slipped out to find an ATM. There, I got another shock. My bank account had only $12,000 left. NFL players don't get pay checks in the off season, and I had many big bills coming due. My car payment, my condo rent in Charlotte, how was I going to make it?

When I returned with cash to cover our dinner bill, Kelechi must have seen the look on my face. Later, when we were alone, I admitted the truth, and he was stunned. He knew the size of my signing bonus and contract.

"What could've happened to that much money?" he asked.

I listed the many deductions from my checks, including hefty taxes and the $10,000 deduction the League takes out for my 401k. But that wasn't the whole story. Frankly, I hadn't kept track of things. I had no experience managing money, and I didn't realize I'd run my credit card up to the limit.

So I went back to living as I had before, spending as little as possible. I kept in training, completed the last of my course work, and graduated from Vanderbilt with a B.S. in Human and Organizational Development. By July, I had only $4,000 left in the bank, and when the Panthers' training camp started and I finally got my next pay check, I felt the skies were clearing. Unfortunately, I was wrong.

CHAPTER TWENTY-NINE

Slowing Down Is Not Part Of My Plan

It never crossed my mind that I would be cut.

All through the summer of 2006, I ate and slept with the Carolina Panthers' playbook, and when preseason started in August, I knew the plays inside out. I'd memorized not just my own parts but the entire D-line and secondary parts, too. I played in all four preseason games, and when we faced the Steelers, I performed so well that All-American Julius Peppers told me, "You're not a 'bubble' guy anymore. You're in. You have nothing to worry about."

Although an NFL player can be released at any time, most of the cutting occurs toward the end of preseason. It's a tense, brutal time. At team meetings, you see the worry in people's faces, and you know they're waiting for that tap on the shoulder. Once, I was speaking to a guy sitting behind me. I turned away, and when I looked back, he was gone. Somebody said, "Yeah, they got him." It happened that fast.

All through August, I waited like the rest, but by preseason's end, no one had tapped my shoulder, and I was breathing easy. We had three days off, so I booked a flight to Nashville to see my friends. On the morning of my flight, when I went for one last workout, my chart wasn't in the weight room. This was odd, so I asked the strength coach about it. He said, "They want to see you upstairs."

Right then, I knew. Wide receiver Steve Smith had overheard, and he stopped me for a minute. "You worked your ass off, man. I saw you get better. I'm proud of you." Then he added, "This isn't your fault. A lot of guys get cut that shouldn't be, and some are kept on that should be cut."

When I went upstairs, Coach Fox gave it to me straight. "We have to release you, Haye. You did a good job, but the numbers didn't work out."

I nodded and mumbled something.

"You're young and talented," he said. "We feel sure you'll be picked up elsewhere. It's harder for older guys with families to bounce around, you understand?"

I don't remember how I answered. Getting cut rocked me hard. You can't appreciate the magnitude of the feeling till you've personally experienced it. Back in the locker room, defensive end Mike Rucker saw me crying and said, "I love to see those tears of joy."

When I shook my head, he said, "Ah no, they didn't!"

Julius Peppers came and gave me a hug, and Steve Smith said, "We appreciate your effort." Somehow, I managed to say goodbye to my teammates. Then I left.

When the initial shock wore off, the feeling that replaced it was anger. I'd had a great preseason, and management had let me believe I'd made the team. It was like being sucker-punched. I'm ashamed to admit, I wanted revenge. My plan was to become a star player on another team, then crush the Panthers and show them how wrong they'd been to release me.

The next day, September 3, 2006, the Panthers listed me on the "24-Hour Waiver Wire." When a player with fewer than four NFL seasons is released, other NFL teams have a chance to claim him on the waiver wire under the terms of his original contract. Just as in the draft, the team with the worst record gets the first chance to claim, and from July through December, the claiming period lasts only 24 hours.

When I called my agent, Jack Sharf, he knew before I even spoke. "Jungle, please don't say it's so."

"Yeah, they got me," I said.

"Don't worry. You'll be claimed," he assured me, and he was right.

Two teams wanted me, the Cleveland Browns and the Tampa Bay Buccaneers. The Browns had the worst record, so they got me. The next day, I flew to Cleveland. When I met the general manager, he said, "We've been watching you for a long time. You're going to be a big part of this team."

His words soothed my battered ego. I thought, wow, they've got plans for me. Once again, I had made "the 53," and soon, I would be able to show my talent. I decided on the spot to make Cleveland my home. Since my contract was still in force, I was making good money, so I rented a nice apartment and bought three big-screen TVs on my credit card. Dad offered to fly to Charlotte and pack my belongings in my truck, then drive up and help me settle in. Clear skies, I thought. The next day, I started practice with the Browns.

Cleveland's stadium was located downtown, but the training facility was in a suburb called Berea. The facility sat in the middle of a residential neighborhood with only a six-foot wooden fence for security, and people would hang over the fence and yell profanities the whole time we were practicing. Sometimes, our ball would fly into someone's back yard. It was a strange set-up.

My first week with the Browns, I did so well in practice that one guy told me, "Man, you're pushing too hard. You gotta slow down."

But slowing down was not part of my plan. Since I'd missed the Brown's training camp, I had to learn their playbook on my own, so I focused on about forty of the most important plays. I hit it hard and really crammed. The Browns had a game scheduled for that Sunday, but since it was my first week, I wasn't surprised when the coach told me I would not dress. The following week, when two D-linemen were injured, I thought they would definitely put me in the next game.

Then, out of the blue, the Browns signed a new defensive back, and that meant they had to release one player from their 53. After just nine days, I was cut again.

This was the worst. Released twice after just one year – how could this happen? On the surface, my record looked like a disaster, and when the Browns put me on the waiver wire after such a short time, no team wanted to touch me. That made me a free agent, and my only option was to sign with the Browns' practice squad. I feared my career was ending.

When I called Dad, I was hyperventilating. I told him not to bother driving my stuff to Cleveland, just to put it in storage. I moved out of the apartment into an Extended Stay hotel, and I also returned all three TVs. I didn't know how much longer I'd have a job.

For seven weeks, I worked on the practice squad, the low point of my life. I didn't travel with the team, and when they played, I didn't sit on the bench. I dreaded getting questions from the press. The worst part was in the locker room before the game. As we marched out to the field, the team would go right, and the practice squad would go left. That crushed me.

Sometimes I called my brother Mike, but it was hard to talk to him because he was hurting for me. My parents were worried, too. Cleveland was cold, dreary and miserable, and Berea felt like a wasteland. The practice schedule prevented me from going anywhere else. Mostly, I hung out in my hotel suite.

Frankly, I thought I was too good for the practice squad. I saw it as a joke, and I was deeply embarrassed by what others might think. But the truth was, God was testing me. Every day, He gave me the freedom to give up on my dream, but every day He was asking, how much are you willing to go through to get what you want?

Many times, I called my agent for career advice. Jack Sharf had really courted me prior to the NFL draft, paying my way to football games, putting me up in nice condos, taking me to fine restaurants, and giving me gifts. But now I rarely saw him, and he didn't always return my calls. Nothing seemed to be happening with my career. I thought about going to Los Angeles to try a career in modeling or acting, but that didn't feel right. I couldn't quit football without proving myself. I simply had to get up and try again.

Finally in week five, I made the decision to find another agent. Jack seemed to understand that I needed to go a different way, and we have remained friends. After we parted ways, I called Sean Kiernan, an agent with Impact Sports. Sean had offered to represent me before, and after watching my career for two years, he'd made his offer again. He told me I belonged on the field, and I just needed a chance to prove it. Sean had graduated from Vanderbilt, started as an assistant agent, then worked his way up the ladder. He wasn't as flashy as Jack Sharf. He was more basic.

As I listened to Sean's pitch, I felt he'd been standing by my side all along. For me, Sean was the right choice. One short week after hiring Sean, he called to say, "Pack up, Jovan. You're going to the Tampa Bay Buccaneers."

CHAPTER THIRTY

Defeat Is A Great Teacher

From Cleveland to Tampa Bay – what a contrast. In a matter of just a few hours, I was back among the palm trees, ocean breezes and warm sun, in weather that was tailor-made for football. How lucky I felt that I had not given up on my dream. As soon as I joined the Buccaneers, I got the one thing I had been needing, a chance to perform on the field.

The Bucs played outstanding football. Coach Jon Gruden had led the team to a Super Bowl championship in 2002, and at that time, he was the youngest coach ever to achieve that honor. Defensive coordinator Monte Kiffin was considered by many to be the greatest defensive coordinator in the NFL. I met them both on the first day.

Their brand-new $30 million training facility was built like Fort Knox. It was secluded among trees near a lake, and during practice, they would drape the fences so no passersby could see us. It was the only facility I'd seen with state-of-the-art hot tubs and cold tubs. There was also a players' lounge, a game room with pool tables and video games, and a sports medicine clinic. The stadium lay just across the parking lot.

I arrived in late October, 2006, the middle of the season, and as usual, I felt jittery about fitting in with a new team and learning a new playbook. In Carolina, we'd watched a lot of film of the Bucs, and I admired how they played defense. Instead of using gimmicks, they relied on straightforward agility and power. The team had strong veteran leadership, and many of their younger players were talented beyond belief. I didn't play the first week, but after that, I played every game.

What really impressed me about the Bucs was how unselfish the veterans were about teaching what they knew and pulling the younger players along. The Bucs were everything a team should be. They celebrated each other's successes with dozens of choreographed gestures and moves. Even Monte Kiffin celebrated.

Kiffin had an expression, "rowing the boat," which meant we had to pull the oars together as a team. In a game with Chicago, we were getting killed, and when we finally turned the game around, Kiffin did the "rowing the boat" gesture on the sidelines. Every official's flag went down, and when we were penalized for celebrating, Coach Gruden just shook his head and smiled. Another time I did a cartwheel and got a fifteen yard penalty. While I was there, our team received dozens of penalties for celebrating. I loved it.

Also, the team socialized like a family. Guys would bring their wives and kids. We'd have cookouts at each other's homes, meet up at the mall, go to the kids' birthday parties, do charity work, share the holidays together. If a teammate didn't show up, we'd call and bug him.

On top of that, I was living near my family again, and I got to see my brother Mike more often. He attended all my home games, and his support meant the world to me. Tampa was so different from Cleveland. There were thousands of restaurants, clubs, movie theaters and entertainment complexes. You'd see parents and kids out walking at all hours, old people and young, skateboarders, cyclists, street performers. You'd hear music and laughter on every corner. It was as if I'd flown from purgatory straight up to cloud nine. In every photo of me in Tampa, I'm smiling.

At the ripe age of twenty-three, I thought of myself as a fully mature adult, but I was soon to discover an important lesson in humility. Being cut from the Panthers had wounded my ego, and I wanted revenge. The Bucs played in the same division as Carolina, and we would face the Panthers twice each season. So I made plans to get even.

Not only did I resolve to perform so well that they would regret their decision to cut me, but I also began to insult their players on the field. I started talking a lot of crazy trash, trying to shake them up. That really annoyed their coaches and infuriated the team. At the time, I didn't realize how my behavior actually degraded me more than anyone else.

Then one day I ran into my old friend Thomas Davis, the Panthers' linebacker. We were in the hotel lobby the day before a game, and I said, "Tell 'em to get ready."

Thomas shook his head. "You have to let that go, Jovan. The players didn't have anything to do with your release."

His words made me realize how immature my behavior had been. I wasn't the first person to be cut from an NFL team. It was just business, but as a rookie, I'd been too inexperienced to understand. Thomas Davis helped me see that holding onto an old resentment showed a lack of dignity.

"You're right," I told him. "I shouldn't have done it."

He and I have remained friends, and after that talk, though I continued to play as hard as I could, I showed the Carolina Panthers more respect.

By the end of my partial 2006 season with the Bucs, I'd made seventeen tackles. The year 2007 was better still. I started all sixteen games and was twice nominated as NFL Defensive Player of the Week. I also received four "game balls" in 2007, the locker room award given by the team to its most valuable members after a win. I finished the season with ninety-seven tackles and six sacks. Best of all, our team made it to the playoffs.

Our wild card playoff game against the New York Giants was the first and only time I started a playoff game. All through the regular season, a team's goal is to make it to the playoffs, but as I'd discovered before, when you achieve your big dream, the level of intensity only goes higher. Our focused preparation leading up to the playoff game was much more concentrated than in the regular season. We were one of only twelve teams in the nation still practicing, and we knew that when we played, the world would be watching. Even my relatives in Jamaica would see my performance. That magnified the pressure.

As January 6, 2008, approached, my stomach felt tight. We were ranked higher than the Giants, but they'd already proved they could hang with the record-setting New England Patriots, and they had the momentum of the underdog coming from behind. It's an indefinable quality I've witness many times before and since, a powerful desire to win that drives a team to victory, despite the odds. The Giants had struggled through their season, and they'd barely made the playoffs. They couldn't afford to feel comfortable. They were not favored to win. I read the sports news constantly, and so did my teammates. When the media says you have the better team, you believe it. We felt confident.

That Saturday was a magical day. We were in our own stadium in Tampa, and the zipline cameras were rolling, ready to catch our every move. We played well, and more than once I hit the renowned quarterback, Eli Manning. Several times, we were in position to put that game out of the Giants' reach, but we missed our opportunities. They recovered faster than we did from turnovers and bad calls. Maybe it was their long struggle, their need to prove something, that made them so hot. They beat us 24 to 14, and our game launched their winning streak that would carry them all the way to an upset victory in the Super Bowl.

It's rare that an undefeated team wins the Super Bowl, because defeat keeps you humble and makes you work harder. It forces you to feel yourself, to recognize your weaknesses as well as your strengths. When you have to keep pushing against obstacles, you eventually build up an unstoppable momentum. I've seen this in my own life. The obstacles I've faced have made me stronger.

CHAPTER THIRTY-ONE

I'll Just Be Who I Am And Do What I Can Do

After the 2007 season, my contract with the Bucs expired, and they offered me a long-term contract. Though I sincerely wanted to stay, rumors were flying that the coaching staff might soon be fired, and my agent and I felt we could get a better offer elsewhere, so I declined. That made me a "restricted" free agent – meaning that, since the Bucs had made me an offer, they would have the right to match any other team's offer and retain me.

The Buc's management placed me on a first-round tender, or in other words, they assigned me the same value as a first-round draft pick. That was a high mark of respect. Finally, my talent had been recognized, and it felt like a confirmation. But in the real world, it meant another team would have to trade an actual first-round draft pick to get me. That was unlikely, and sure enough, it didn't happen. So the Bucs got to keep me for one more year.

I embraced that outcome. I was in the best shape of my life, playing at my highest level, and making serious money. Tampa had always been good to me, and I had great expectations for the coming season. My agent said 2008 would be my "contract year," the year on which my career-high earnings would be based. Yet 2008 turned out to be a rough year – partly because I pushed myself too hard.

I'd always been strong and fast, but I wanted to gain more flexibility. So that summer, I added an intense stretching routine to my off-season workouts. The trouble was, I overdid it. I didn't realize how the extreme stretching would destabilize my muscles. The first week of training camp in Orlando, I'd caught a bug, and I was ill with a fever and nausea. Yet I didn't want to show weakness, so I took my position on the scrimmage line facing two players across from me, a "double team." As soon as we clashed, I felt a slicing pain. My groin muscle had been torn.

Man, it was excruciating. The general manager rode with me to the clinic, and he said, "Whatever Jovan needs, see that it happens." That's how much he valued me. Still, the injury caused me to miss the entire training camp, a major setback. When the regular season began, I started the games wearing a wrap and playing through pain.

Then in our first game, I pulled a ligament in my left thumb and had to wear a thumb splint for the rest of the season. I couldn't grab anything. I'd become a one-handed player. Just a few weeks later, an opponent stepped on my right foot and tore my lisfranc ligament. For four weeks, the team doctor gave me horse-size shots of cortisone, and my foot hurt for the rest of the year.

It didn't end there. We were playing New Orleans when an opponent hit me hard and twisted my knee. On the next play, the opponent pushed me back twelve yards, and I couldn't do a thing to stop him. My knee was popping in and out of joint. I'd sprained my medial collateral ligament. That injury caused me to miss our Monday Night Football game with Carolina.

I watched that game on TV, propping my achy knee on a cushion. "What have I done? Haven't I been living right?" I asked.

My brother Mike said, "God's testing you. How strong will you be?"

That game was the only one I missed all year. The coaching staff had no pity when it came to pain. But the truth was, if Monte Kiffin had told me to jump off a cliff, I would have honestly considered it. All the defensive players felt that way. He was almost like a dad to us, and no one wanted to let him down.

The year was mostly a blur, but I started fourteen out of fifteen games, and I do remember one game in particular. We were facing the Atlanta Falcons and their quarterback Matt "Matty Ice" Ryan, who was the 2008 Offensive Rookie of the Year. Our game was scheduled for the Falcons' stadium in Atlanta, and I got tickets for Kelechi, Moses, and a few of my other Nashville friends. "Be ready for a show," I told them.

On game day, the stadium atmosphere was festive, and the Falcon fans were buzzing with energy. Nevertheless, we packed our defense and dominated the field. After every advance, we celebrated as a team. We didn't need a crowd to cheer us on. We had a huge win, and the team rewarded me with another game ball.

After the game, Kelechi said, "Y'all are some fools. I've never seen a team celebrate that much. Everything you told me was right."

At last, the 2008 season came to a close, and I'd recorded thirty-three tackles. Despite my injuries, it was not a bad year. But the rumors proved true, and both Jon Gruden and Monte Kiffin left the Buccaneers. The team wasn't the same after that, so in early March, I became an "unrestricted" free agent, and that weekend, other teams started calling my agent with offers. I would have played for Gruden and Kiffin the rest of my career if things hadn't changed.

The NFL Free Agency window officially runs from early March to mid-April, and free agents are signed in three waves. The first wave includes players most in demand, and they get the best financial offers. In the second and third waves, the offers decrease in value with each passing day. I received three contract offers in the first wave, confirming how much my NFL stock had risen while I played with the Buccaneers.

Interest came from the Seattle Seahawks, the Houston Texans, and the Tennessee Titans. The Titans were offering serious money. If I'd had a better 2008 season, they might have offered more, yet it was enough to give me financial security and the means to help my family. The only thing left was to decide which team to join. Before, when I'd been drafted or picked up on a waiver, I'd had no control over where I would go. Now for the first time, I could make my own choice.

That first weekend, while my free agent offers were still coming in, I decided to fly to Nashville and talk to the Titans. My agent Sean Kiernan and I had worked out a strategy to let the Titans know I was interested, but that I also had other offers. While I was there, I met the general manger, the vice president, the scouts and the coaches. D-line coach Jim Washburn took me to lunch, and I heard the head coach Jeff Fisher tell him, "Don't let Haye leave without signing."

All day, I was back and forth with my agent on the phone while he negotiated my contract. I toured the Titans' training facility, which was smaller and older than others I'd seen. Still, I liked the Titans' defense and strong coaching staff. Also, I felt comfortable in Nashville and still had many friends there. It felt like coming home.

The Titans offered me a four-year, $16 million contract, and that Monday morning, I signed it. That same afternoon, we held a press conference. I'd attended media events before, but this was the first time national reporters came just for me. They asked a lot of questions, and I felt stressed, but also ecstatic.

Defensive tackle Albert Haynesworth had just left the Titans, and the reporters wanted to know how I would replace him. Haynesworth was an All Pro. He'd been a first-round draft pick, and he surpassed me in both height and weight. The pressure to fill his shoes was intense.

I answered their questions with the honest truth. "I can't replace Haynesworth. I'll just be who I am and do what I can do."

Later that week, I moved to Nashville and took a suite at an extended stay hotel. Tennessee was cold that time of year, and right away, I missed the warmth and life of Tampa. I missed racing jet skis with my teammates and cooking out on the beach. Nashville was a quieter city, with only small pockets of street life. In fact, that's one reason I chose it over Houston or Seattle. I knew my lifestyle would slow down, but that was okay. I was nearly twenty-seven, and I wanted to find a wife and start a family. In Tampa, I'd seen players bringing their wives and kids to barbecues and picnics, and I thought that was the sweetest thing.

Also, since growing up in Jamaica, I'd always enjoyed the countryside. I'm not cut out to live on a farm, but there's a lot of open space and parkland around Nashville, with picturesque green hills, lakes and streams. I welcomed that.

CHAPTER THIRTY-TWO

If You Can't Be Happy For The Next Guy,
You're Not Enjoying The Game

Titans' football, at least during my time there, was as different from the Bucs as night and day. Head Coach Jeff Fisher and D-line Coach "Wash" Washburn rotated players in and out of the game more often than the Bucs did. While in Tampa, I had played close to 80 percent of the time, and I never got tired. Our passionate fans turned our stadium into an adrenaline factory, and once we found our rhythm, we didn't need to stop. I was the number two D-lineman in the league for playing the most snaps, so it's no wonder I often finished games with tackles in the double digits.

By contrast, the Titans didn't have such an impassioned "twelfth man" in the bleachers cheering us on, and the coaches believed that resting the D-linemen between plays gave them more energy. This didn't prove true for me. I found that sitting out only interrupted my momentum and lowered my statistics. Since I participated in less than half the plays, I finished my first Titans season with 55 tackles and my second season with 52 tackles, quite a drop from my performance in Tampa.

The rotation philosophy wasn't the main difference, though. In Tampa, we would have done anything for Coach Monte Kiffin, but the Titans showed less respect for their coaches. Kiffin congratulated every player who made a contribution, whether it was knocking off a blocker or taking down a double team so a fellow player could tackle the ball carrier. Kiffin knew it took eleven guys to make a winning play. He got the best from his players. By contrast, the Titans coaches only acknowledged the one man who made the tackle. Contributing didn't count.

I often sensed tension and jealousy among the coaches and rivalry among the players. A lot of guys were too concerned about how much money the next man made. Our D-line coach hardly ever hung out with the other coaches, and we had little back-and-forth communication. Also, the Titans didn't socialize much as a team. It was rare to see them playing cards or sharing home-cooked meals or asking about each other's children.

This may sound like a trivial thing, but our practice locker room was not a big open area as most are. Instead, the space was divided by a wall of lockers, and that made a subtle difference in how the team interacted. We couldn't talk and joke together, and it was harder to form relationships.

As a result, the offense and defense didn't mix, and during games, the guys didn't congratulate each other for big plays, much less celebrate on the field. I seldom saw helmet butts or chest bumps. It was all about individual glory.

When the guys asked me why I cheered for plays I hadn't made, I said, "If you can't be happy for the next guy, you're not enjoying the game."

That was the crux of the problem, I think. The Titans in those days had many outstanding players, but they'd lost their pure love of football. In time, I realized that, for many of them, money and personal fame were the only priorities, and the definition of team camaraderie was heavy partying. Since I didn't drink alcohol, some of my teammates considered me "lame."

I had never been one to seek the spotlight, and though I certainly enjoyed the financial rewards, money was not my only focus. While in Tampa, I used to pay an older teammate $500 every time he sacked a quarterback because he made less money than me and I wanted to encourage him. It was all about being part of something bigger. In that respect, the Titans were a disappointment for someone of my nature.

Nevertheless, the move to Nashville brought me an extraordinary blessing. About four months after I arrived, I met my future wife.

At first, I'd been so focused on fitting into a new team, learning a new playbook and also shopping for my first house that I didn't have time to think about socializing. I

bought a house in May, and when I wasn't practicing football, I was moving furniture and setting up my new living
quarters. That June, when a teammate asked me to join him
at a nightclub, I almost said no.

Still, I got a haircut and laid out some clothes, just in
case, and at the last minute, I decided to go. A couple of
players were meeting at Karma, a popular Nashville night
spot, and it just so happened that the organizers of a local
charity event were having their after-party celebration at
Karma that night. As I was climbing the stairs to the club
entrance, I noticed a small, slender woman in line ahead of
me. Something about the way she moved caught my attention. When she turned around to speak to her friends, we
made eye contact, and I saw that she was beautiful. Also,
she was white.

Since my childhood crush on Stacy Ann in elementary
school, I had dated a white girl only once. That girl was
friendly enough, but we had so little in common and our
conversation was so awkward that I told myself, Never
again. Consequently, although this blond, blue-eyed girl
on the stairs was lovely, I turned my attention elsewhere.

In the club, I was sitting with linebacker Keith Bulluck,
and we were talking football when this same woman came
rushing past us. She waved and said "Hi" to Keith, and then
disappeared in the crowd.

"Who was that?" I asked.

"My home girl," Keith said.

"Home girl, what does that mean?"

He laughed. "She's a good girl. We're just friends."
He told me her name was Jennifer Maynord.

She passed us several times. She seemed very busy,
and I later learned that she had planned the charity event
and was now handing out gift bags to the people who had
attended. My head kept turning her way. When I tried to
get her attention, she said, "I'll come back."

Finally she had a moment to stop by our table, and
Keith introduced us. There was just something about her
energy and her lively smile. I was captivated. I'd never
known what to say to a white girl. What I said to Jennifer
that night was, "I'm going to marry you some day."

CHAPTER THIRTY-THREE

What If I Never Saw Her Again?

Of course, Jennifer thought I was joking about marriage, and when I asked for her number, she gave me her business card more as a courtesy than an invitation to call. I stuck her card in my pocket and didn't think about it again till I got home. I was just getting undressed when I realized her card was missing.

Man, I hunted all over my house for that card. I checked and re-checked my pockets. I looked under the furniture. Where had I dropped it? What if I never saw her again? I spent half the night searching.

The next morning, I checked my car, and there it was. It had slipped into the crack between the driver's seat and the console. My relief was so intense that I called her right away. "Would you like to catch a movie? Maybe grab something to eat?"

She seemed in a hurry. "I'll have to call you back."

What could I possibly say to a white girl? I didn't know. I was operating on instinct. That night I called her again, and we talked for three hours. It turned out we had a great deal in common. Like me, she was a homebody who'd grown up in a small town surrounded by a large extended family of church-goers. She told me all about Sparta, Tennessee, and I told her about Toll Gate, Jamaica.

She was also a hard-working entrepreneur. She'd started out as a flight attendant, then owned a nail salon, and now she owned a party planning business while also working at a law firm. I admired her drive. I wanted to own a business myself one day. Talking to Jennifer was easy.

I mentioned that my birthday was coming up in a week, and she said, "Are you free that day for lunch?"

My first impulse was to shout "Yes!" But I couldn't. An old girlfriend was driving in from Atlanta to spend that weekend with me. I'll just call her Jane.

Jane and I had been dating off and on since our freshman year in college, and when we first met, I thought she was the one. Many times, we'd broken up, then gotten back together, and she used to say, "No matter who you're with, you'll always find your way back to me." But Jane had a way of dangling me like a fish, reeling me in, then casting me off. When she needed something like free tickets to a game, she was all sweetness. But when my career was bottoming out in Cleveland, she wanted nothing to do with me.

My brother didn't like her, and once when we were staying in her house, he slept in the car rather than spend a night under her roof. But since I'd landed my Titans contract, she was being sweet again, reeling me back. So I told Jennifer that I'd have to let her know later about a birthday lunch.

Soon after that, my old friend Kelechi asked if I had birthday plans, and I told him about my dilemma. "Maybe I can see them both," I said.

He threw up his hands. "Why are you doing this? Jane's no good for you. She treats you like dirt."

"But she apologized and wants to get back together," I said.

Kelechi was firm. "You can't juggle two girls. You have to choose." Then he warned, "If you cancel on Jennifer, she may never see you again."

His words touched a nerve. Jane had hurt me many times over the years, but I still felt the old tug of fondness for her. On the other hand, Jennifer treated me with warmth and kindness. My birthday fell on Sunday, and after waffling back and forth, I finally accepted Jennifer's lunch invitation, still hoping I could find a way to see both women on the same day.

Jane arrived on Sunday morning. She called me as soon as she reached the Nashville city limit, and I met her in front of a bookstore near Vanderbilt. She'd brought me a card, a small gift, and a cake. The first thing she said was, "Why couldn't we meet at your house?"

"I won't be there today," I said. "I'm probably going out with the guys later."

She wouldn't accept that excuse. "Why is it a problem for me to stay at your house?"

Finally I told her, "I'm going to see another girl."

Jane exploded. She cursed and called me names. "You made me drive all this way!" Next she started crying. "You can keep the cake and gift," she said. "I don't want them."

Her outburst made me feel terrible. I'm not a spiteful person. I should have saved her that drive from Atlanta, but I'd taken too long to decide. When I tried to soothe her, she pushed me away. She didn't want to hear my apologies. Finally, I just left. As bad as it was, I knew our break-up was for the best. Afterward, I shared the cake with Kelechi and some other friends, and we ate every crumb. That cake was delicious.

Then I called Jennifer, and we met for a late lunch at a Mexican restaurant called the Cantina. To my surprise, she brought her best friend along. Okay, I understood. She didn't know me, and there's a stigma attached to pro football players. People think we're surrounded by glamorous women and that we take women out only for sport. I guess Jennifer felt a friend would give her security. Nevertheless, we talked and had a good time, though we kept the conversation impersonal.

When I invited her to drop by my house that night, she said, "Maybe another time." I could see she wanted to take things slowly.

That night, we spoke on the phone another three hours, and the next day, we called each other several times. Later that week, she finally came to my house for dinner. We got some take-out, watched a little TV and talked. She told me she'd dated black guys before, and I was glad to hear it. But later, when I asked if I could stop by her house, she said, "No, my sister's visiting with her family."

That wounded me. "You don't want me to meet your relatives?"

Jen smoothed things over. She said, "I really like you. I just don't want to get my hopes up too soon."

Two weeks later, we were texting every morning and seeing each other almost every night. Usually we met at my house for dinner. I had a movie room, and we both enjoyed sharing quiet evenings at home. We'd get take-out, or Jennifer would cook. I discovered she's a fabulous cook. Best of all, Jennifer made time for me. She was so easy to be with.

But there was also another reason why we mostly stayed in. The first few times we went out in public, I was very conscious of people's reactions. Black women especially gave us bitter looks and whispered to each other. Waitresses became frosty, not all of them, but some. Excessive anxiety has followed me all my life, and with so many reports of hate crimes on the news, I began to worry that we might be shot. Once we were walking along holding hands when a lady deliberately bumped into us and gave us a scowl.

"Did you see that?" I asked Jen.

Since Jen had dated black men before, she was more used to people's reactions. She said, "Are you afraid to go out with me?"

"No, of course I'm not," I said.

"You're always talking about it. Does being with me make you uncomfortable?"

I took her hand. "Jen, I want to be with you."

But the disapproval on strangers' faces bothered me, and it took me a while to adjust. I knew my attitude weighed on Jennifer – so much that I began to fear I might lose her. I sent flowers to her office, also Teddy bears, chocolates, and other small gifts. Still, for a long time, we steered clear of certain places, or we just stayed in.

Then in July, Jen took me to her home town of Sparta to meet her parents. I also met her brother and sister and her sister's family. Though she'd dated black men, she'd never taken one home, and I was really uncertain what to expect. Not many black people lived in Sparta, and I wondered if I was going to encounter rednecks. When we first arrived, I sat bolt upright on the living room couch, afraid of making a mistake.

We started talking, and in just a few minutes, I began to relax. Jen's family was very down-to-earth, friendly and welcoming. Her mom worked as a court reporter, and her step-dad was an electrician. Her brother played basketball and loved sports, so he and I had plenty to talk about. Her family didn't know I played with the NFL until Jennifer mentioned it. We stayed with them all weekend, and everyone got along well.

These days, I adore Jen's family, and we visit them often. They take me hunting for deer, turkey, and doves, and they worship our two daughters. I've never felt anything but warmth when we're with them.

I knew that the meeting with my parents would be a different story.

At that point, I hadn't told Mom and Dad about Jennifer, but I knew that when football season started, they would fly up to see my games, and inevitably, they would meet her. I told my brother first that I was dating a white girl. His reaction was typical. He didn't care, as long as I was happy. Finally, I called home and spoke to Mom. Her reaction was typical, too.

"Why a white girl? Why don't you stay with your own kind?"

I'd grown up hearing that sentiment. Dad especially used to tell me that if I married "outside my race," I would be letting my people down.

"Mom, I really like her," I said, "better than anyone I've ever known."

She was quiet for a moment. "Did you tell your dad?"

"You tell him, okay?" I said.

"He won't be pleased."

After that conversation, I knew their upcoming visit would be an ordeal.

Before long, Jen began to stay over at my place, and soon she was spending more time at my house than at her condo. In all the years I'd dated the other girl, Jane, I never gave her a key to my home. I didn't think twice about having one made for Jen. I trusted her. I kept saying I wanted to marry her, but she always just laughed.

"I know you have a wife somewhere," she'd say. "You're just not wearing your ring at the moment."

"No way," I said. Everything I wanted involved Jennifer, but I still needed to prove to her that I meant it.

That summer, I treated Kelechi, Moses and myself to a long weekend in Toronto, Canada. We had fun seeing the city and enjoying the night life. I met many beautiful women, but all I could think about was Jen. I kept my cell phone with me every minute, even in the bathroom, because I didn't want to miss her call. Once I had to leap out of the shower to answer, and my phone got drenched. That weekend, I rang up a $900 phone bill, and Kelechi said, "Aw man, you've already fallen for that girl."

That's when I knew for sure.

In September, as football season approached, I asked Jen to move in with me, and she accepted. Shortly after that, my parents and brother arrived to attend our first home game. Jen picked them up at the airport and took them to my house, where I was waiting. She cooked a nice meal for them, and she was cordial and attentive. Really, she was just being herself. My dad usually didn't speak much. He preferred to stay in the background. But that day, he talked constantly to Jennifer.

Brother Mike pulled me aside and said, "Dad kind of likes Jennifer. He may just forget about you and me."

That made me smile. Jen had stolen Dad's heart. Mom was a bit more reserved, though. She didn't talk much, and I couldn't read her reaction. She had a way of smiling just to hold people off. Actually, I really didn't care what Mom or anyone else thought about the woman I loved. I'd already decided to marry and have children with her.

In any case, their visit went much better than I'd expected. Mike called me after they got home and said, "Dad talked about Jennifer the whole trip. He said she's just what you've been needing."

Later when I talked to Mom, she was less enthusiastic, but she said, "If Jennifer makes you happy, then it's okay with me."

One year later, on September 18, 2010, Jen gave birth to our first daughter, Jorielle LeShay Haye. Ten days after that, we got married. I had proposed to Jen repeatedly, but she always thought I was teasing. In the spring of 2010, I had decided to convince her.

First I called a jeweler friend to design an engagement ring. Then I planned how and where to propose. We had never been a traditional couple, and neither of us were the extravagant type. I decided to propose on Cinco de Mayo, May 5th, in the place we both loved best, our home. To set up the evening, I bought a dozen small gifts, including a card, a rose, chocolates, a pair of shoes, and so on. I placed the first gift in the garage where she'd find it as soon as she got home from work. Then I hid the others all over the house, with a clue attached to each one hinting where the next gift might be found.

The ring didn't arrive till the day before Cinco de Mayo, and on top of that, one of the diamonds had fallen out. So I had to scramble to find a jeweler who could repair it in time. But by the time the momentous evening arrived, I had everything ready. Jen came home, found the first gift and the clue, and she loved the scavenger hunt idea. It was the sort of thing we often did for each other.

I followed her through the house as she searched for more surprises. Sometimes I had to help her find them. The second-to-last gift was upstairs in our movie room, and after she opened it, she turned around and found me kneeling at her feet with the ring box in my hand.

She burst out laughing.

"Jen, be quiet. I'm trying to propose."

As soon as she realized I was serious, she started crying. We hugged and kissed, and to my happy surprise, the ring actually fit her finger. She spent the next half hour making phone calls, telling everyone our news. Then we went out to a Mexican restaurant to celebrate.

Our wedding was just as unconventional. We felt no rush to marry, and we both expected to put it off a few years. Then one day, soon after Jori was born, I said, "Let's do it the day after tomorrow," and Jen said, "Why not?"

We got married in front of our own fireplace, with Jen's parents, the judge and his wife, and Jen's best friend as our only witnesses. Jen wore blue jeans. I wore basketball shorts and flip-flops. Afterward, we packed up little Jori and went to the Cheesecake Factory for our honeymoon. When I told my teammates about our ceremony, they couldn't believe how plain it was. For Jen and me, though, it was perfect.

CHAPTER THIRTY-FOUR

We're Best When We're Running And Flying To The Ball

My personal life was as good as it gets, but my career was headed for more bumps.

On January 27, 2011, just after my second Titans season ended, the management let Coach Fisher go and fired his staff. To replace him, they promoted their offensive line coach Mike Munchak to the head position, and they brought in a young guy named Tracy Rocker as the new D-line coach. This would be Rocker's first year coaching pros, and he was on a mission to stir things up. That spring, the Titans drafted three new D-linemen, each younger than me by almost a decade. Suddenly I was "on the bubble" again, and I knew I'd have to work hard to make the roster.

First, Rocker wanted bigger guys on defense, and he told me to add weight. He set my goal at 330 pounds. In Tampa, we never had specific weight goals. Kiffin just wanted us to be strong and fast. Normally I carried about 270 to 290 pounds, and I felt good that way, able to move with speed and agility. But I didn't want to give the Titans a reason to cut me, so I started eating more. When I was training hard, I could easily lose ten pounds a week, and I worried about that during my off-season workouts. Sometimes I didn't push as hard, and every day I drank extra protein shakes to pack on the pounds. Yet all that extra bulk felt like dead weight.

A greater challenge for me was learning an entirely different stance. My extreme right-handedness had continued to limit my stance, but Monte Kiffin had said, "Don't change your stance. You're comfortable as you are. Just practice moving your right foot as fast as possible." D-line Coach Rocker was not so accommodating. Instead of taking a sprinter's stance, with my right heel off the ground ready to spring forward, Rocker wanted me to stand with my feet parallel and both heels flat.

After six years of playing pro football, I could drop into my old stance in a heartbeat, but I had to stop and think about how to arrange my feet for the new stance. Worse, the new foot placement didn't give me the same speed and power as before. Often during practice, I would revert to my old stance, and Coach Rocker would yell at me. It took me three weeks to adapt.

Added to that, Rocker used a different defense system. I'd always been a solid "3-technique" player, meaning that I aligned on a gap in the opponent's offensive line, facing the shoulder of the man opposite me and defending the gap against any offensive play. This gave me flexibility to read the other team's formation and play my opponent either tight or wide as needed. But now, Rocker wanted me to play tight on my opponent at all times, regardless of their formation. This often left my gap undefended, which gave the other team an advantage. Although I tried to explain the strategy we'd used in Tampa, Rocker was not interested.

In preseason, the rookie D-lineman got much more time on the field than the "older vets." I played part of three of games, and though my efforts often disrupted the opponent's entire play, I didn't make many tackles myself. Still, I was always happy to see young players doing well. Once when I was celebrating a rookie's great play from the sidelines, Coach Rocker couldn't believe it. "Why so much emotion, Haye? You didn't make that tackle."

"This is football," I said, "I'm just happy to be here."

I've never been disrespectful to a coach, but at that moment, I realized that Rocker's view of football was not the same as mine. When he looked at my stats, he said my production was down. He failed to take into account that I'd participated in fewer plays. The truth was, I was Coach Fisher's guy, and the new staff would never see me as one of their own.

A couple of days later, I was coming out of the locker room when a scout called my name. "Coach Munchak wants to see you."

This time, I felt no overwhelming emotion at being cut. Coach Munchak thanked me for all my hard work, and

I thanked him for the opportunity. He said the younger guys were progressing really well, and I knew he needed to free up some money to pay their salaries. I accepted the news, got my papers signed, picked up a few personal items, and left. To this day, I cheer for the Tennessee Titans and wish them all the best. I owe them a huge debt of gratitude for recognizing my talent and giving me financial peace of mind.

My brother Mike, who has always been my biggest fan, wrote me a letter which I treasure. Here's what he wrote:

Dear Big Bro,

We both know the last two years weren't what you expected or wanted them to turn out on the field. Well, it's a new year, and the past is the past. You been working hard the whole off-season to better yourself, and now the time has come for you to show it.

The past is the past, but you can't forget or won't forget the feeling you had not dressing. You should have that drive every day in prac-tice and bring it through the season. It's a team sport, but now you have a family to provide for. A new daughter and a wife to play for. We all are behind you.

God knows how much I want you to be selected to the pro bowl and more. I know that you have the skills and the heart to take you over the top. You're back at the weight you were, and now you just have to get things rolling. The best Jungle is the one running and flying to the ball, having fun.

I would just love to hear your name be discussed among the elite DT's in the current game, and I know you're capable of doing it, cause you have proven everything else to me. If you have a bad day, push yourself to have a better one. In the next Madden, your rank will be 90. Let's go!

I'm predicting an injury-free season, 36 tackles, 7 sacks, 2 fumble recoveries, 1 interception, and your career touchdown. I really believe it. I'm going to continue praying for you every night. Love you, big bro. Put things in God's hands, and he'll take good care of you. Look at you now.

> *Love always,*
> *Lil Bro*

CHAPTER THIRTY-FIVE

God Wrote Me A Different Script

There's a time and a season for everything.

For a while after leaving the Titans, I flew around the country, doing tryouts with various NFL teams, including the Chicago Bears, the Detroit Lions, and my old team, the Bucs. The anxiety I felt about flying only added to the pressure I was feeling about my career in the NFL. Through the years, my phobia had worsened, until just the sight of the airport would give me sweaty palms, a hammering heart, and vivid images of crashes. I had to take medication to keep my panic under control. Otherwise, I'd be overcome by dizziness, shakes, nausea, tunnel vision, and the absolute certainty that I was about to die a horrible death.

As much as I disliked all that airplane time, I gave it my best shot whenever an opportunity came my way because I loved football.

In December, 2011, an All-Pro defensive tackle with the Detroit Lions got suspended, and the Lions signed me up to replace him. I played one game, and out of seven plays, I made two tackles and a quarterback pressure. The general manager said, "That's pretty good for a guy off the street." But four days later, their All-Pro returned, and they dropped me. Less than a week after that, the Tampa Buccaneers offered me a two-year contract. It sounded good at first, but their coaching staff was about to leave, and I didn't want waste a whole training camp and then get stuck with a new staff who might release me.

Football had been my life. But I was realizing that my future might hold an exciting prospect that had nothing to do with the game I loved.

Back in 2006 when I first lived in Tampa, I had met Juan and Ramon Alvarado, two brothers who owned an upscale jewelry store and did custom designs for a lot of my teammates. We'd become friends, and they were the ones I called to design Jennifer's engagement ring. Ramon was the salesman, very energetic and persuasive, with a natural instinct for marketing. Juan had a degree in Information Technology, and he was one of the smartest people I'd ever met, always reading and analyzing the economy. When the recession hit, their customers stopped buying expensive jewelry, and after a while, the brothers decided to sell their store.

In 2010, they had approached me with a new marketing concept, an online exchange of new and used goods and services for small businesses. Because I respected their business sense, I listened. Numerous people had asked me to finance various entrepreneurial ideas, but Juan and Ramon had already test-marketed their concept online and the response was good. They'd received inquiries from fifty-nine different countries.

Each time I met with the Alvarados to discuss the company, I grew more enthusiastic about its potential. I talked the idea over with Jennifer and Kelechi. Kelechi usually played devil's advocate, but when he heard the details, he said, "I think it could work." Jennifer's response was positive, too. So I started out in 2011 with a small investment.

I was still with the Titans when I became partners with Juan and Ramon, knowing my football career wouldn't last forever, but not expecting it to end the way it did.

Detroit called me one more time. They had an injured D-lineman, and they needed me to play replacement again. But I had a meeting scheduled that week with Juan and Ramon, and suddenly I realized that launching my new company excited me more than a chance to play one more game of football.

I could have continued trying out, and maybe another team would have offered me a contract. My friend Kelechi asked, "What do you want most?" When I told him I was more fired up about my new company, he said, "Okay, you've made your decision. Call your agent now."

Jennifer was pregnant with our second child, but she wasn't worried. She said she'd support me in whatever I did. My decision felt right. In early 2012, I called Sean Kiernan and told him I was retiring from football.

That week, I flew down to Tampa to meet with my partners in our new enterprise. We made plans to support online auctions, barter and classified listings, all fully integrated with social media such as Facebook, Twitter, LinkedIn, Google+, and others. Using the site would be free, and we'd earn revenue by offering added features for a small fee and by running pay-per-click ads on the site. Compared to our big-name competitors, we intended to deliver more functionality at lower cost.

What appealed to me most was our mission to help small businesses save money. Small business is the foundation of our economy, and our site would help hard-working entrepreneurs find bargains on the items they needed. I felt very good about this mission because I'd always believed God blessed me so that I could help others.

Sometimes I see guys still playing football who never came close to my numbers, and I'm happy for them. I wanted to play stellar college football, enter the NFL as a first-round draft pick, dominate the field from day one, and then end my career in a Pro Bowl. But God wrote me a different script.

Before postsharesell.com, I had held only one paying job, professional football. One of the best side benefits of that job was the opportunity to support charities. I am thankful that I can offer financial support to worthy causes, and I've learned that giving my time is important, too. I remember that first visit to the hospital when I was in the flutophone choir. It makes me smile now, recalling the trouble I had playing the flutophone, but the sick people just enjoyed having us visit. To this day, I love to visit hospitals and talk to sick people, trying to cheer them if I can.

Maybe my own struggles have made me more sensitive to the sufferings of others, but there's definitely something in it for me when I "give back." The gratification that comes from charity work is priceless, whether it's serving meals in family shelters, driving vans full of children on field trips, buying books for needy schools, speaking to kids with learning disabilities, or supporting children overseas. Jennifer and I are always thinking about ways to give back. We talk about sponsoring a Pee Wee football team for kids who wouldn't otherwise have the opportunity to play, because the Pee Wee leagues are where you really find that pure love of the game, or even adopting a couple of underprivileged children ourselves. You can see why the service mission of postsharesell.com attracted me.

All the lessons I learned in Human and Organizational Development at Vanderbilt are coming back to me now. Ramon, Juan and I think the same way about supporting and serving our users. We don't want to be one of those companies that starts overcharging customers, taking shortcuts on service, and exploiting our own employees to maximize profit. We have a different model in mind. We want to give back to our customers and employees in every way we can.

Recently, we ran a $100 cash giveaway on our site, and a coffee shop owner won the prize. At first the woman didn't claim the money because she thought there had to be a catch. When we finally convinced her there were no strings attached, she posted a blog praising us. She also passed the money on, giving each of her customers a free cup of coffee that day. That's the kind of success story Juan, Ramon and I want to see.

All three of us share the same title, Founder and Co-CEO, because we don't like hierarchy. We all share in the planning and brainstorming. Juan takes care of IT, Ramon handles marketing, and I work with our attorneys to manage the legal end. To keep overhead low, we outsource the other functions for now, and so far, it's been a magical experience. Every time we need a certain skill or connection, the right person appears. We've already found a seasoned publicist, who is also a specialist in social media integration and a guy with years of experience in online barter. We've expanded our database three times due to rapid growth, and we're now building our own proprietary software.

Things are moving fast. When we launched postsharesell. com in January, 2012, we had just a handful of users, but in four months, we were averaging over 100,000 daily site hits and close to seventy new user sign-ups per day. That same month, on April 12, 2012, Jen gave birth to our second precious daughter, Jaiana Lizzy Haye. Could my life get any better?

At the age of thirty, I'd be a fool to pretend I know everything about business, and there's no doubt I'll be tested again. Maybe I'll face defeat and have to start over, but I've learned how to do that. Every day, I can't wait to get up and start working because, once again, I've become part of something bigger than myself. Just as the power of a great dream carried me all the way to the NFL, so I sense the same power will drive me to succeed in this new arena. I may be naive, but I'll keep trying harder, learning new lessons, giving more effort. The obstacles I've faced have strengthened my determination and made me more certain that I can win. Maybe that's been God's script for me all along.

JAMAICA

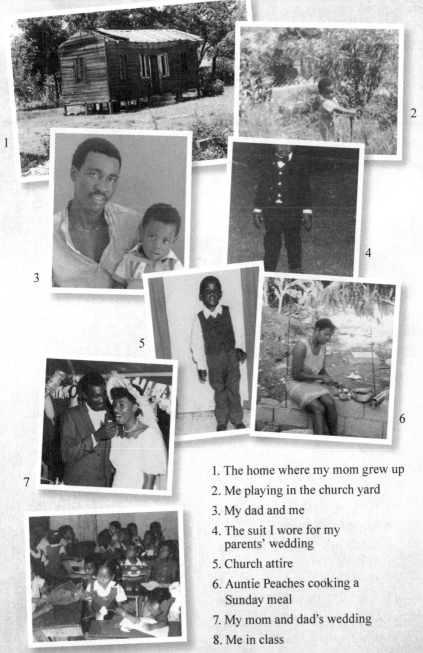

1. The home where my mom grew up
2. Me playing in the church yard
3. My dad and me
4. The suit I wore for my parents' wedding
5. Church attire
6. Auntie Peaches cooking a Sunday meal
7. My mom and dad's wedding
8. Me in class

9. First day of school
10. Me and my cousins
11. Auntie Peaches washing dishes in our kitchen
12. More dishes
13. Auntie Cynthia and her daughter
14. Michael's birthday party
15. Standing on a relative's grave

NEW JERSEY

16

17

18

19

20

21

16. Playing in the circle

17. Me, Michael and Mom in front of our apartment in Cliffside Park

18. Dinner time in the kitchen

19. The family getting ready for church

20. Family photo

21. My grandmother on my mom's side

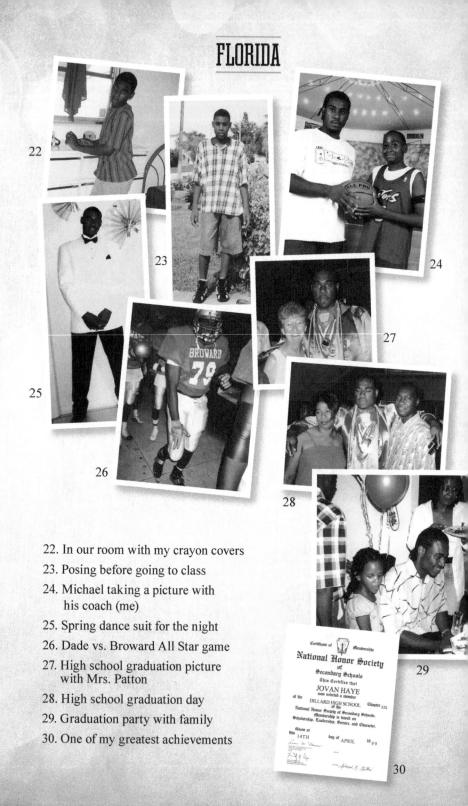

FLORIDA

22. In our room with my crayon covers
23. Posing before going to class
24. Michael taking a picture with his coach (me)
25. Spring dance suit for the night
26. Dade vs. Broward All Star game
27. High school graduation picture with Mrs. Patton
28. High school graduation day
29. Graduation party with family
30. One of my greatest achievements

31

32

33

34

35

31. Nigel and me on moving day

32. My rookie debut card

33. My college playing card

34. College graduation picture with my parents

35. A still picture of me doing what I do best

36

38

39

36. Tampa Bay Buccaneer head shot
37. Another big hit on a division rival
38. My NFL Future rookie card
39. Me in Titan blue

FAMILY

e PostShareSell.com⁴⁶

40. Me, my wife, the kids and Nana and Papi

41 My life!!!

42. Me, Michael, Mom and Dad

43. One great family picture

44. My business partners Juan and Ramon, I love these guys!!!

45. A great night for a wedding

46. The next billion dollar company

THE END